TWAYNE'S WORLD AUTHORS SERIES
A Survey of the World's Literature

Sylvia E. Bowman, Indiana University
GENERAL EDITOR

BRAZIL

John P. Dyson, Indiana University, Bloomington
EDITOR

Graciliano Ramos

(TWAS 324)

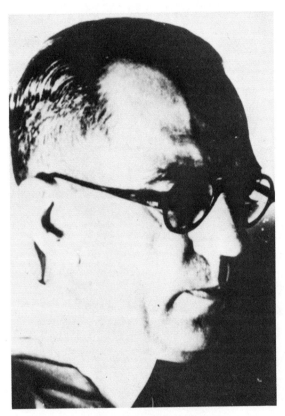

Graciliano Ramos

Graciliano Ramos .

By RICHARD A. MAZZARA
Oakland University

Twayne Publishers, Inc.   ::   New York

Library of Congress Cataloging in Publication Data
Mazzara, Richard A.
  Graciliano Ramos.
  (Twayne's world authors series, TWAS 324. Brazil)
  Bibliography: p. 121.
  1. Ramos, Graciliano, 1892 - 1953.
PQ9697.R254Z72   869'.3   74-6227
ISBN O-8057-2741-8

Contents

About the Author

Richard A. Mazzara, Professor in the Department of Modern Languages and Literatures of Oakland University, Rochester, Michigan, is a specialist in the Romance field. He received his B.A. (1948) from Queens College, Flushing, New York, an M.A. (1949) from The Johns Hopkins University, and the Ph.D. from The University of Kansas. Professor Mazzara has published numerous articles on the major Romance literatures in leading professional journals. He first became interested in Portuguese and Portuguese-language literatures in 1962 at the University of Texas, where he held an NDEA Post-doctoral Fellowship. In 1963 he was an NDEA Fellow also at the Luso-Brazilian Center of the University of Wisconsin and had an OAS grant to do research in Brazil in 1964. Subsequently, Professor Mazzara has initiated programs in Portuguese and Latin American Area Studies at Franklin and Marshall College, Lancaster, Pennsylvania, and Oakland University. Although he continues to teach French and Spanish as well as Portuguese, his principal areas of research and publication are the modern Brazilian novel and theater.

Preface

Graciliano Ramos (1892 - 1953) was outstanding among Brazilian writers engaged in a new cultural mission starting in the 1930's. Somewhat apart from the mainstreams of Modernism and Regionalism because of its author's age, location, and temperament, his work reveals from the beginning a happy blend of regional and universal elements. Graciliano, unlike many of his fellow Northeasterners and other compatriots, always favored celebrated European novelists of the Realist and Naturalist movements as models. It was in these largely traditional molds that he poured his own very personal materials, often autobiographical in whole or in part. Nor should the great Brazilian novelist Machado de Assis be overlooked as an important model, although contrasts between the two writers are as significant as comparisons.

Consequently, Graciliano escapes both the picturesque excesses typical of regionalists of all ages and the linguistic eccentricity that characterizes Modernists. His work develops subjects and themes on the individual as well as on the collective levels, in forms that are classical in the best sense of the word. Graciliano has left a faithful portrait of modern Brazilian life with all its problems. Meticulous and vigorous in his art, he re-creates the human scene more than the physical landscape, sometimes showing the influence of the latter on the former, sometimes the interpretation by the human of the physical surroundings. Like other modern and contemporary writers, Graciliano depicts the decadence of a ruling class, in particular that of his native *sertão* (drought-ridden backlands), but avoids the trivial of so much Regionalistic literature. Above all, he emphasizes the result on individuals of the contrasts and conflicts of Brazilian life in his time, very much including himself both as author and actor.

Ironically, the "discovery" of Graciliano Ramos and the publication of *Caetés* in 1933 made him a Modernist. He seems to have felt obliged to adhere somewhat to the artistic and political tenets of the movement. Having been drawn out of his relative isolation, Graciliano produced his best novels, although not necessarily his most significant or authentic work. He was not comfortable with the Modernists' sometimes studied negligence in linguistic matters, nor with "Socialist Realism." His use of down to earth language is always appropriate and formally correct. Although it is as valid to interpret Graciliano's works "sociologically" as it is to so interpret those of his fellow Northeasterners, his writings are better classified as "psychological" whether they are autobiographical or not. The realism of the best of them results from artistic distillation rather than from any doctrinaire attitude.

Before presenting Graciliano as a man and a most personal artist, despite appearances, it seems appropriate to indicate his place in literary history. I have referred to Graciliano as a Modernist, however marginal, and shall therefore summarize the chief characteristics, and compare him with other writers, of the movement here.[1] Brazilian Modernism began in São Paulo in 1922 and lasted through several phases until 1945. One offshoot of the movement that was also a reaction to it, Northeastern Regionalism, is important because Graciliano's participation in it, although still marginal, was somewhat greater.

Modernism in its beginnings was principally an aesthetic and cultural revolution. Its objective was to break down a colonial mentality in art and letters that largely ignored national realities in order to imitate foreign currents in these areas. It did not intend to limit itself to São Paulo nor to art and letters, but to embrace the whole nation and integrate activities in every sphere. It was successful in bringing about a vast transformation in Brazilian life through studies in the arts and sciences, particularly the social sciences. In theory and practice the great leader of Modernism from its inception to its close was Mário de Andrade, whose death in 1945 coincided with the end of the movement. There were more talented authors than he, yet none so significant in shaping Modernism.

The movement not only modernized Brazilian thought and action, but made a more integrated Brazil known to the world. The nation became liberated, independent at the same time that it continued to adapt foreign materials, and able to contribute to world culture. Regional culture, traditions, folklore, and language, including the contributions of the principal races of Brazil, took on new national meaning for Brazilian intellectuals who revitalized them in their works, whether creative, scholarly, or critical. They no longer felt cultural or intellectual life was impossible away from the metropolis, whether Rio de Janeiro or Lisbon, and many preferred to remain in their native states rather than move to the capital as before.

There was constant emphasis from the beginning, not only on the independence of Brazilian letters, but on the aesthetic value and autonomy of a work of literature. Most of the numerous polemics of Modernism dealt with questions of form and technique rather than content, with the result that later Brazilian authors, perhaps more *engagés* than their elders, have generally been marked also by greater professionalism than they. Another important question was that of developing linguistic studies and a Brazilian Portuguese suitable for literary purposes. The growth in number and quality of secondary schools and universities throughout Brazil has been in large measure both the cause and effect of this concern with language and literature as a discipline. On the one hand, the time of amateurism or dilettantism of authors for whom literature is a youthful or leisure occupation has passed. On the other, Modernism has been a breath of fresh air to Academism. Despite the problem of making a living, still a great one for writers in Brazil, more of them have devoted their talents and energies exclusively to their work than in the past, when other occupations or peripheral literary activity took most of their time.

A certain reaction against Positivism, the materialistic philosophy that prevailed in Brazil during the nineteenth century, in favor of more spiritual values, placed emphasis on the reform of poetry during the first phase of literary Modernism. After 1930, however, the reform spread to prose fiction. The novel and short story had undergone considerable transformation through the Romantic and Realist periods, but it was the revolutionary spirit and experimentalism of Modernism that brought them out of the sphere of European influence and made for uniquely Brazilian expression in these as in other genres. As regards content, much progress had been achieved to incorporate the Brazilian scene by various nativist movements such as Indianism. In fact, except for the psychological novel, most Brazilian literature was Regionalistic. Whether rural or urban in nature, however, this literature tended to show man determined by his environment, in keeping with the Naturalism which was then in vogue. In the case of the psychological novel, Symbolism and Impressionism were the predominant European influences. Modernism was to serve as the necessary catalyst to produce something new of the several "-isms" with which Brazilian novelists had already experimented. The result was a more nationalistic Regionalism, sometimes propagandistic as in the early Jorge Amado, sometimes documentary as in Lins do Rêgo's "Sugar Cane Cycle" or Amado's later works of the "Cacao Cycle." Usually allied to the regional in urban centers, the psychological novel continued to develop as with Erico Veríssimo or, especially, Graciliano Ramos. As for the short story, Modernism abandoned the well-made type à la Maupassant for evocative, impressionistic, slice-of-life pieces such as Graciliano composed. Again, it took some time for formal and linguistic problems to be resolved satisfactorily. The Brazilian *crônica,* a subjective reaction to some current event or situation, much like the American newspaper "column" or informal English essay, has been one highly satisfactory solution, despite its somewhat circumstantial, transitory nature. While Modernism has tended to avoid the historical and the concrete for the spontaneous and spiritual, it has sought to develop works of lasting, universal value.

Modernism was by no means a completely unified movement, but for the first few years all reactions and counterreactions were centered in São Paulo. Then two related but different Modernisms developed in other parts of the country. The first was Regionalism, beginning in 1926 and having its home in Recife, and the second the "Testa" or Spiritualist group, dating from 1927 in Rio de Janeiro. Both were traditionalistic and conservative, especially the second, which was Catholic in inspiration and hostile to the men of São Paulo. The one had as its chief goal to base Modernism more soundly on cultural traditions, principally those of the Northeast, the other to structure its aesthetics along more classical lines. Neither goal corresponded very well with those of Modernism, which gave rise to numerous polemics. While Regionalism remained largely unknown outside of Recife, the second group, having originated in the capital, gained national fame immediately. Both had elder statesmen, Gilberto Freyre and Tasso da Silveira, respectively, each of whom longed to be the Mário de Andrade and to establish the dominance or priority of his group. Regionalism is, of course, the only one of these submovements of any relevance to a study of Graciliano Ramos.

In later years Gilberto Freyre and his followers pretended that Regionalism dated from 1923 in order to minimize the priority of Modernism. He was not referring to precursors; if he had, he might very legitimately have had Euclides da Cunha in mind, whose *Os Sertões* (Rebellion in the Backlands [1902]) is to the backlands what *Casa Grande e Senzala* (The Masters and the Slaves) is to the littoral. It is true that Freyre returned to Brazil in that year after studying and traveling in the United States and Europe, and that he met José Lins do Rêgo in that year. The latter was part of a small group in Recife that had begun to acquire some vague notions of Modernism under the leadership of Joaquim Irojosa, and Freyre too joined the group. The young sociologist was by no means the leader of the group at that time, which may partially explain why he did not take to Modernism enthusiastically. In fact, the movement was not generally acceptable to the traditionalist intellectuals of the Northeast. Some became converts in time, such as the poet Jorge de Lima, but many, including Graciliano, retained a certain distaste for Modernism. It would be several years, however, before Freyre was to formulate the principles on which to base a movement that might parallel and oppose that of São Paulo. Moreover, it would be many years before Freyre or Regionalism became widely known in Brazil. Indeed, as a sociologist and Regionalist Freyre was more revolutionary than traditionalist. This latter characteristic has become more pronounced with the passage of time, as has the rivalry between the Northeast and the South.

The fact is that Modernism was as badly known in Recife as what would develop into Regionalism in São Paulo. By the time that Modernism reached the Northeast it had abandoned its purely aesthetic approach and already acquired some political direction, Leftist or Rightist, depending on the sect. Between 1925 and 1927 Modernism appeared to be Leftist, and the men of Recife saw a real need to reaffirm the cultural values of the Northeast. Nevertheless, the Modernists were still very fundamentally concerned with literature and the fine arts, while the future Regionalists emphasized culture in a broader and more popular sense, e.g., cookery, crafts, and the like, for some time to come. The birth of a modern Northeastern literature therefore owes at least as much to São Paulo in its initial stages as to Recife. Regionalism and Modernism were complementary, after all, differing only in degrees of traditionalism and cosmopolitanism. Yet Regionalism was elaborated by Freyre chiefly as an anti-Modernism, in large part to prove its independence. Its negative, combative attitude, however, actually made it quite dependent on Modernism.

Regionalism was in fact to enjoy its most brilliant period in the 1930's and 1940's with the flowering of the Northeast novel, which by and large followed a program already proposed by the Modernists in 1922. These had accomplished a literary revolution; the Northeasterners were most significant members of a group in

Brazil devoted to accomplishing revolution through letters. The nationalization of literature and its consequences during the ferment of the 1920's made a number of Northeasterners adhere to nationalistic political parties of either extreme as readily as it did the Paulistas. Modernism depended heavily on Regionalism to achieve its program of nationalization. In politics as in literature, differences were rooted in forms much more than in content. Some of the best writers were dedicated to social reform, and therefore inclined to Communism. In protest their heroes were often beaten and apathetic, much like Graciliano's protagonists. Others, less interested in reform than in developing the nation, tended toward Fascism. Their heroes were usually idealized athletic types, virtually nonexistent in Brazil in those days. Brazil needed a strong man then as throughout its history. He would be Getúlio Vargas, notably with the Estado Nôvo from 1937 - 1945. His form of Integralism compromised the extremes by means of a "Leftist" program for the people in the framework of a Fascist dictatorship to protect the middle class that benefited most from the program.

Gilberto Freyre (1900 -) did not wish to represent Modernism, and his work owes little to the movement in conception and nothing in style. Yet *Casa Grande e Senzala* does meet the sometimes vague goals and corresponds to the spirit of Modernism. Despite his independence and hostility, Freyre gave form and concrete meaning to the instinctive understanding that the Paulistas had of Brazil but could themselves express only in a poetic way. *Casa Grande e Senzala* further modified Modernism in the 1930's, and all the production of the Northeastern novelists before and after it coincides with its systematic treatment of the cultural history of Brazil. His success was so great because Brazilian intellectuals had been prepared for him through considerable discussion, a variety of essays of several persuasions, many by Modernists, and especially by the Regionalist Manifesto of 1926. He was read for a wealth of scientific information, subjectively interpreted, a certain crystallization in form, and a highly personal style. Influences were mutual, then, and the chief difference between Freyre and the Modernists was his nostalgia for the past and their forward-looking attitude. He has continued to become more conservative with age.

An important politician as well as an author, José Américo de Almeida was an immediate precursor of the great novelists of the Northeast. In a sociopolitical treatise he dealt with the ills of Paraíba and suggested remedies on the model of *Os Sertões*. The popular novel *A Bagaceira* (Sugar Cane Trash [1928]), concerned with the problems of *sertanejos* displaced to the littoral by the drought, is sociologically sound and moving despite discrepancies between the realistic content and often romantically artificial style. In the 1930's revolutionary enthusiasm and hope grew stronger, and the social novel with its sociological approach was attuned more than before to political developments. A critical spirit and rugged style akin to Euclides da Cunha's caused the problems of Brazil to be set forth realistically in the new novel, but also made clear to public and government what was needed to resolve them.

José Lins do Rêgo (1901 - 1957) had good reason to be in sympathy with Modernism. He believed in free expression, social themes, and above all the regional basis. Yet there was one important contradiction: he was primarily a memorialist, not only looking to the past, but to a declining society and degenerate individuals, while the Modernists generally turned optimistically to the future. Perhaps still more than in Graciliano's, memory plays a greater role than imagination in his works, with the best, most representative ones based very directly on his experience. Accordingly, his first novel, *Menino de Engenho* (Plantation Boy [1932]), is almost literally repeated in *Meus Verdes Anos* (My Green Years [1956]), the first volume of his memoirs. Moreover, these explain much of the "Sugar Cane Cycle" novels. In this searching of the past, as in his feeling of being lost and abused as a child in a decadent society, Lins do Rêgo closely resembles Graciliano. His heroes are like their society that cannot view the establishment of large corporate sugar mills in the same light as the rest of a progressive, prosperous Brazil. Although destined to great success in literature, they, as well as Graciliano's protagonists, are failures in the everyday life so well documented in that literature. However important and popular in their day, Lins do Rêgo's novels are now less than universal in appeal, doubtless because of their virtues as much as their defects. Scarcely more than a storyteller, very much in the tradition of the Northeast, he offered also the social document that was then felt to be sorely lacking in Brazilian letters but that now tends to date him.

Jorge Amado's (1912 -) work ranges from almost pure Communist propaganda (*O País do Carnaval* [Carnival Land], 1932) to Bahian Regionalism with a political message ("Cacao Cycle" novels, 1933 - 1946) to academic literary art on a sociological, regional foundation (1958 -). All of his work is marked by the author's basically romantic nature. Like the other novelists of the

Northeast, Amado became a Modernist in spite of himself, as a student in Bahia condemning the nationalistic, Leftist political tendencies of São Paulo and proposing alternate reforms. Moving to Rio de Janeiro, however, he soon became involved in the literary and political revolution of the 1930's and turned inevitably to Modernism and Communism. Deficient as a writer and thinker in his first works, he was saved by his instincts, spontaneity, and the primitivism of his style, Modernist qualities that continue to prevail in his novels. Ironically, he has never completed what was to be his great political novel *Os Subterrâneos da Liberdade* (Freedom Underground). Further, his first consciously Modernist novel, *Seara Vermelha* (Red Party [1946]), is a poor one and came at the end of the movement. Unconsciously, he had prepared for his first superior work, *Gabriela, Cravo e Canela* (Gabriela, Clove and Cinnamon [1958]), in some of the novels of the "Cacao Cycle" in the 1940's.

Rachel de Queiroz (1910 -) understandably began her career with a social novel, *O Quinze* (The Year '15 [1930]), the story of the terrible drought of 1915. Although much of the content reflects the author's experience in her native *sertão* of Ceará, her works are in no way memoirs. Entirely objective sociologically speaking, *O Quinze* is warm and tender, yet without sentimentality, from the human point of view. There is no political message, and the style is sober. Unlike Graciliano's *Vidas Sêcas* (Barren Lives), however, Rachel's concentration on the suffering of one family tends to neglect adequate development of the plight of *sertanejos* as a group. Her presentation of the role of women in the *sertão* is equally objective but personal, too, colored by as well as based on her own experience, particularly a frustrated maternal instinct. Subsequent novels, such as *João Miguel* (John Michael [1932]) or *Caminho de Pedras* (Rocky Road [1937]), deal similarly with themes of the downtrodden in the *sertão,* imprisoned murderers, prostitutes, and proletarians of all classes. Although the note of social protest is strong on occasion, Rachel's novels are always novels, never political tracts like those of the early Jorge Amado. Like Graciliano, she is primarily interested in individual psychology as in *As Três Marias* (The Three Maries [1939]), in her case especially of feminine characters, and the search for truth in solving universal human problems. Like Graciliano, too, she prefers the loose structure of short, near-independent chapters, general conciseness, and language derived from natural speech. Perhaps because Rachel has produced few novels, they are of uniformly high quality, as are the many short narratives and *crônicas* that she continues to write.

At first the critics, including some from São Paulo, sometimes accused the sociological novel of excessive monotony and depression in so relentlessly depicting the life of the proletariat. Nevertheless, Modernism and the South were being outshadowed by the literature of the Northeast. The Paulistas themselves recognized the richness of the new social themes, for, as Freyre pointed out, the problems of the Northeast were essentially those of Brazil and all of Latin America. During the repression of Communists and their sympathizers in 1935 - 1936, Jorge Amado was arrested and forced into exile, Graciliano imprisoned, and even Gilberto Freyre detained and physically attacked on several occasions. Public and government alike had been apprised, whether explicitly or implicitly, of what was required to solve the problems. With the Estado Nôvo, however, censorship became stronger, and the proletarian literature was declared to promote disorder and therefore to be immoral. Social themes subsequently became less important, with little or no propaganda, and psychological studies were emphasized more. Enemies of the dictatorship, Jorge Amado, Rachel de Queiroz, and Graciliano Ramos stopped publishing for a while. Amado's later works, no longer propagandistic, are far superior artistically to his first novels. Rachel relegated the political to the status of background material, concentrating on the psychological and becoming noted for her portrayal of the Brazilian woman of the Northeast. Graciliano's sociopolitical content, on the other hand, had always been "disguised" in his fundamentally psychological novels; his short narratives and memoirs followed in the same vein. The only famous Northeastern novelist to work continuously through the Vargas regime, Lins do Rêgo pursued the sociological far less and tried his hand at a variety of themes until his death. It is interesting that, despite its repressive measures, the Vargas regime had some salutary effects on the work of three of the four important novelists of the Northeast, and curious that Graciliano did not elaborate on this irony. Interesting, too, but not curious is the fact that the demise of Mário de Andrade and Modernism came in the same year, 1945, as that of Getúlio Vargas and his regime.

Always dissatisfied with himself, as with everything else, Graciliano not only polished and repolished his comparatively scant work, but constantly experimented with ideas and forms. Most critics agree that he was successful; a few say that he was correct to feel frustrated, that he never realized his potential. I am inclined to believe that, insofar as anyone ever realizes his full potential, Graciliano did. The study of his best known and most representative writings will reveal to what extent the sum as well as each part of his work is successful. A more important revelation is that the wide range of experimentation of his relatively short career permitted him to triumph over circumstances and return to dealing with himself as the protagonist of his work, directly, on his own terms as a human being and as an artist.

Oakland University   RICHARD A. MAZZARA

Chronology

For a more detailed chronology, see Rolando Morel Pinto, *Graciliano Ramos, autor e ator* (Assis, 1962), pp. 177 - 82.

1892   Born in Quebrangúlo, Alagoas, son of Sebastião Ramos de Oliveira and Maria Amélia Ferro Ramos, the first of many children.

1894   Family moves to Buíque, Pernambuco.

1900   Family moves to Viçosa, Alagoas.

1904   Founds and directs *Dilúculo,* a newspaper for children.

1905   Enters secondary school in Maceió; publishes his first sonnets under a pseudonym.

1910   Family moves to Palmeira dos Indios; Graciliano works in his father's store.

1914   Goes to Rio de Janeiro; works as editor on several newspapers; begins writing short stories.

1915   Returns to Palmeira dos Indios upon learning of the deaths of several members of his family from bubonic plague. Marries Maria Augusta Barros and opens a drygoods shop.

1920   Graciliano's wife dies, leaving him with four children.

1925   Begins writing *Caetés.*

1926   Becomes President of the School Board in Palmeira dos Indios.

1927   Elected Prefect of Palmeira dos Indios.

1928   Marries Heloísa Medeiros; four children will be born of this marriage. Finishes *Caetés.*

1929 - Writes two reports to the Governor of Alagoas.

1930   Resigns as Prefect to become Director of the State Printing Office; moves to Maceió and collaborates on several newspapers.

1931 - Resigns this last office, returns to Palmeira dos Indios, and

1932   founds a school. Writes *São Bernardo.* Has a serious operation.

1933   Appointed Director of Public Instruction in Alagoas. *Caetés* is published by Augusto Frederico Schmidt. Graciliano begins work on *Angústia.*

1934   *São Bernardo* is published by the Ariel Publishing Company.
1936   Imprisoned in Maceió and transferred to Recife and Rio. *Angústia* is published by José Olympio, wins the "Lima Barreto" Prize of the *Revista Acadêmica.*
1937   Released from prison. The *Revista Acadêmica* dedicates a special issue to him.
1938   *Vidas Sêcas* is published by José Olympio.
1939   Appointed Inspector of Secondary Education.
1940   From this year until his death Graciliano is engaged in a variety of literary activities. He writes, principally short stories and memoirs, translates works from English and French, is translated into Spanish and other languages, and participates in literary conferences. He receives several honors.
1945   Becomes a member of the Communist party. *Infância* is published by José Olympio.
1947   *Insônia* is published by José Olympio.
1952 -   Graciliano and his wife travel in the U.S.S.R. Upon his
1953   return he becomes very ill, is operated on, and dies less than a year later. The *Memórias do Cárcere* are published posthumously by José Olympio, as is *Viagem* (1954). (Other works are reedited by other publishing houses.)
1961   *Obras Completas* are published by Livraria Martins.

Brief Summaries of
Graciliano Ramos' Novels

THESE four works will be discussed several times from different points of view. It is therefore wise for the reader to have résumés of them at the outset. Their plots and exterior action are slight. Two additional major works by Graciliano will be discussed at length also. It is impractical, however, to summarize *Infância* (Childhood) or *Memórias do Cárcere* (Memories of Prison) other than to say that the first is a collection of episodes based on the author's memories of childhood, and the second, equally episodic, his recollections of prison life during 1936 - 1937.

Caetés: The narrator, João Valério, is a young clerk in the commercial establishment owned by the elderly Adrião Teixeira and his brother in Palmeira dos Indios. He hopes to make a name for himself by writing a novel on the original inhabitants of the region, the Caeté Indians. Another of his ambitions is to become the lover of Adrião's attractive young wife Luísa. Scenes are frequently set at places such as João Valério's boardinghouse or Adrião's house where the narrator's acquaintances meet most often. Descriptions of local types and their preoccupations provide a satirical picture of middle-class society in the city. João Valério succeeds in becoming Luísa's lover. When Adrião hears of the affair, he asks João Valério for the truth. The latter denies it, and Adrião pretends to believe him, but he commits suicide in shame at their accommodation. When Adrião dies after a long agony, the lovers realize that their affair has ended too. João Valério abandons his novel with the further realization that the project is pointless. His society is as cannibalistic in its way as that of the Caetés. The petty love affair is merely another episode in its history. João Valério will marry a young woman well placed in the society of Palmeira dos Indios.

São Bernardo (Saint Bernard): Paulo Honório, the middle-aged master of São Bernardo, a large cattle ranch near Viçosa, Pernambuco, writes his memoirs. He traces his ruthless climb from very humble origins. One day he decided to marry in order to have an heir, but fell unexpectedly in love with the woman who became his wife. Young, a schoolteacher, and humanitarian, Madalena was very different from her husband, and their life together was not happy. Paulo Honório was accustomed to dominating and became insecure when Madalena attempted to take her place as mistress of São Bernardo and put her ideals into practice. When he became jealous of a student, it was not because Madalena had given him any cause, but that he needed a reason for dominating his wife. Madalena finally took her life, and Paulo Honório learned from her suicide letter that she had been faithful. He vowed to respect her last wishes and care for their son. Political and economic disasters befall him as he begins the book which will serve as edification and catharsis for him and his readers.

Angústia (Anguish): In what turns out to be a delirium the narrator, Luís da Silva, gradually apprises the reader of his *sertanejo* background and recent past in Maceió, Alagoas. The picture that he paints of his family and society in the backlands is full of decay and violence. His existence as a minor functionary and hack writer living in a wretched boardinghouse in the city is no less sordid. He led a repressed, solitary, dull life until he became involved with Marina. She did not make him happy, but aroused him sexually, obliged him to propose marriage in order to gratify his desire, and proceeded to spend more money than he had for her trousseau. By the time that he had no more and was in debt, Marina was Julião Tavares' mistress. Frustration and resentment built up in Luís against Tavares, who represented everything that he envied and hated. When Tavares abandoned Marina because she was pregnant, Luís' thought of murdering him materialized. The illness that had long incubated erupted in the crime, to be followed by a delirium that was both Luís' punishment and cure. *Angústia* is the account of the narrator's derangement.

Vidas Sêcas (Barren Lives): The cowboy Fabiano, his wife Vitória, their two sons, and their dog are pursued by the *sêca* (drought) that regularly plagues Northeastern Brazil. As they come upon a deserted *fazenda* (ranch), it begins to rain. The land is immediately transformed, as is typical in the *sertão*. Fabiano and his family establish themselves on the ranch and consider it a time of plenty. Additional episodes in a loosely connected series show the members of this representative family engaged in representative activities, sometimes individually, sometimes as a group. The action is interior as much as exterior. Final scenes depict the inevitable return of the drought and the family's departure from the *sertão*, like so many others before and after them, in search of a better life elsewhere.

CHAPTER 1

The Man in His Work

THERE is a reasonable compromise between extreme critical views. Is the work the man? Or does art exist entirely for its own sake? Surely the work does reflect the man, however tenuously, and it is therefore valuable to have some secondary sources in order to verify to what extent it does. Yet criticism is not exclusively biography, as art is not autobiography alone. A study of Graciliano Ramos' work reveals just how necessary the compromise is, for virtually all of it is the product of a fusion and confusion of goals under various pressures. That the fusion was often deliberate, or at least successful, may be judged by the critical acclaim that Graciliano's work has generally received. On the other hand, a good clue to the degree of confusion experienced by Graciliano himself, and sometimes others, is the author's frequent expression of dissatisfaction, especially with his first works. To be sure, it may be argued that it was his awareness of and efforts to overcome the confusion that permitted him ultimately to achieve greater integrity and success.

In the following quotation from an earlier study of Graciliano's novels, I suggest the evolution that was probably his as an artist and a person:

> . . . São Bernardo, and especially Angústia, might have led him back in time, much as his protagonists are led back. Without investigation of the problem, some have wondered why the novelist sought inspiration in his native region later rather than earlier in his career; others have inquired why he chose Vidas Sêcas as a title for his last novel, when all his characters lead "parched lives." Aside from the obvious references to the sêca, to economic and social injustices, and their effects, there may well be consideration of the characters of São Bernardo and Angústia, who are in fact psychologically more withered by their civilization than those of Vidas Sêcas. Greater cultural complexity tends to produce a higher degree of impersonality, which

only some individuals can be made to perceive and combat by extraordinary means. This tragic-heroic perspective is acquired finally when indifference is shaken and the individual is restored to life and the world. Further on this objective level, one senses a return to an earlier culture, from a more modern to a more ancient conception of heroism and tragedy. In a primitive society there is closer identification between persons and with the environment, and thus the tragedy may be experienced collectively as well as individually. As one moves forward from *Vidas Sêcas,* determinism becomes more impersonal, less a single force to be sensed than a myriad of forces perceived intellectually. May this not indicate that, in the chronological order of living and writing, the artist gradually increased his tragic objectivity on the basis of lesser objectivities? Did this not permit him to write a superior novel on his native region — after writing excellent novels on others — devoid of the neo-Romanticism of which others were guilty?[1]

Although not so well known as *Vidas Sêcas, Infância* is a superior work, not only on Graciliano's native region, but on himself, as are the still more frankly autobiographical *Memórias do Cárcere.* Even more than of *Vidas Sêcas*, a study of these two works illuminates Graciliano's first novels in a very personal way. This is not to detract from *Infância* or the *Memórias* as art, for they too are recreations of a reality that may need to be verified; interestingly enough, such verification may sometimes be made from the novels.

From *Infância*, then, the reader learns a great deal about the early years of Graciliano Ramos, from an affective as well as an objective point of view. One is reminded of the memoirs of José Lins do Rêgo in *Menino de Engenho* (Plantation Boy), particularly in the portraits drawn by the two writers of their grandfathers. Ironically, the weak young protagonist of *Menino de Engenho*, Carlos de Melo, cannot emulate Zé Paulinho, the grandfather who is the center of his life and whom he admires and respects. The grandson of José Lins' work represents the passing of an era as much as he does the memorialist himself. Young Graciliano does identify with his grandfather; more than the passing of an era, both embody a harsh reaction to harsh reality. The grandfather's attempt at self-expression through a craft, the making of plain, sturdy kitchen sieves, and the grandson's through literature, plain and sturdy in its way, are forceful replies to as well as partial escape from injustice and cruelty. The older Graciliano identifies similarly with the protagonists of his first novels who, like him, must busy themselves with more worldly activities in addition to writing. In fact, the life of the protagonist of each of his novels contains elements of Graciliano's, and the author could almost have led any one of those lives. Again, it seems appropriate to quote myself, for what I once said with reference to Graciliano's novels clearly may apply in a consideration of his life:

> . . . in each novel I discern two levels of objectivity. These may be termed the collective level, where Naturalistic determinism presumably reigns supreme, and the individual or tragic, where free will may continue to struggle for survival. While these levels cannot in fact be separated in life or in the arts without oversimplification, one can differentiate and independently emphasize them according to one's purposes. This Graciliano Ramos does, apparently using fate as a means to bring about certain shifts in points of view. His manipulations are subtle, to be sure, for he strives always to maintain artistic objectivity on both levels. They are well worth studying in detail, however, if one is to appreciate the note of hope that our novelist seems bent on injecting into the "parched lives" of his characters, whether they be Brazilians of the Northeast or of the Littoral. It is Ramos' optimistic note, generally overlooked until now, that I should like to emphasize, especially as it seems to be pointed up by a circular structure within each of the novels to be considered and a peculiar chronological relationship between them.[2]

A glance at the chronology will show that Graciliano first left his native Alagoas in 1894 at the age of two. Although one may doubt that the author could recall them at the time of writing, the events of the departure and the trip to Pernambuco seem to be faithfully recorded in *Infância* (1945). In any case, between two and eight years of age Graciliano had the opportunity to become acquainted with another branch of his family and observe that part of the Northeast which, although more favored by nature, still has its droughts. One of these ruined his father's new career as a rancher, forcing him to resume his former occupation of shopkeeper, at first in nearby Buíque, and a short time later in Viçosa, Alagoas. The family seems never to have enjoyed very comfortable circumstances, and hygiene was apparently quite ignored. In both towns Graciliano continued his education, formal and informal, partly in schools, partly at home with his father and other relatives, but mostly on his own. Old-fashioned pedagogy made him detest schooling on the whole, and he must be considered largely a self-educated man.

In addition to that of the grandfather, Graciliano has left memorable portraits of other members of his family and households in both parts of the country. His father was a stern, uncommunicative man, more than a little sadistic and somewhat dishonest in dealing with his family and inferiors. Only some fourteen years older than Graciliano, his mother was occasionally a comrade, but more often a capricious parent. Both thought of him as an ugly, sickly, strange child and often mistreated him. So numerous were his brothers and sisters that none seems to have made a great impression.

Prominent places are given to Emília, a close cousin who died young, and to Mocinha, a pathetic illegitimate sister. Relieving the tragedy of childhood that is *Infância* are recollections of one kindly schoolmistress, some faithful ranch hands, a friendly policeman, a helpful notary, and the black boy who, along with other black and mestizo servants, traditionally finds himself in the world of the white plantation class in Brazil. Another important recollection is that of the popular storyteller in the Northeast whose influence is felt in the anecdotes of *Infância* as in Graciliano's collections of short stories for children and adults.

In general, however, the young Graciliano felt alienated from the adult world by the lack of understanding and cruelty of his parents. Instead of seeking to bridge the gap between the two generations, they persisted in considering him strange, thereby contributing further to his strangeness. Yet Graciliano's estrangement was not without benefit to him or his future readers; for in his isolation he was better able to develop his powers of observation, meditate on his findings, and draw certain generalizations. He became quite bitter and often morbid, not only about his own suffering, but also that of others about him. Possessed of great sensitivity, he was led beyond ordinary misanthropy. For the most part avoiding the sentimentality of romantics of all times, Graciliano at times felt purged by misfortune and succeeded in demonstrating similar catharsis to society through his writings.

Graciliano became acquainted with literature in Viçosa at an early age through the good offices of the few kindly adults in his life, and with their encouragement he began to write. The boy had a short period at a secondary school in Maceió, from which he profited little as from most of his scant formal education. His first efforts at producing literature had been sonnets and, now a member of a literary society where he could practice reading French and learn English and Italian, he continued to write them. After the family moved to Palmeira dos Indios, Graciliano's father took his son to work with him in his new shop. Although forbidden to do so,

Graciliano produced many more sonnets. These he sent under pseudonyms to periodicals in Maceió, where they were published. His success led him to send some of his best work to magazines in Rio de Janeiro, and these sonnets also were printed.

Although Graciliano did not really intend to devote himself to poetry, he was heartened by the acceptance that he had received, and after a family disagreement in 1914 went to Rio to seek his fortune. He found employment on a newspaper, but was most disappointed with the capital and the important men of letters of the day. Returning soon to Palmeira dos Indios, he set up shop for himself, married, and became a respected citizen.

Graciliano Ramos prospered and seemed outwardly to be satisfied with the daily routine of provincial life. His evenings, particularly after his wife died, were, however, given over to insatiable reading. The poems that he wrote gave him a certain feeling for rhythm, but the large, cosmopolitan library that he was acquiring and assimilating was where he received his first real literary training.

Graciliano began to edit and write for *O Indio*, the city's weekly newspaper which was managed by a local priest. During this early phase of his career — reflected in *Caetés*, whose protagonist, João Valério, contributes to a similar publication — Graciliano produced feature articles and columns (*crônicas*), criticizing traditions of all sorts, but written in excellent, most correct Portuguese. Although these writings might well have scandalized the director, they were printed. At the same time, Graciliano kept abreast of the latest literary developments in Brazil, which then meant Modernism. Skeptical of the new writers' work as belles lettres, purist that he was, Graciliano nevertheless recognized that they were trying to produce literature that was more original and more relevant. He felt that the two short novels he had written but shown to no one were dull and lifeless, however pure their language. For one thing, he had not yet attempted dialogue in his work. The Modernists encouraged Graciliano indirectly to try again. Although not the perfect novel, and repeatedly disowned by its author, *Caetés* was to be the result of this new effort and a relative success.

Having acquired a certain reputation as a man of letters, Graciliano was invited by an influential politician from Maceió to head the school board in Palmeira dos Indios. He accepted after some hesitation. Despite his preference for private rather than public life, Graciliano was evidently pleased at having impressed the man from the big city. The new office, time-consuming though it was and carrying no salary, provided another diversion from his business, which was going badly at the time.

His end-of-year report was so impressive that Graciliano was nominated for the position of Prefect of Palmeira dos Indios. Elected to the post, he set about improving the town's poor economic situation, proposing also a new road to connect the town with the backlands. His second report, addressed to the Governor of Alagoas, was so frank that the authorities in Maceió refused to print it, and Graciliano therefore sent it to the Governor in typewritten form. Contrary to all expectations, the report had a positive effect. It was published in two important newspapers, and the Governor and Secretary of the Treasury came to see Prefect Ramos.

These, then, are the two *relatórios* that brought Graciliano literary glory as well as results in his public office. An editor in Rio, the celebrated poet Augusto Frederico Schmidt, imagined that the author of the famous reports might have a novel lying about. Indeed, *Caetés* had been completed three years before, but it was not to be published until 1933. Resigning as Prefect in 1930, Graciliano was appointed Director of the State Printing Office in Maceió. During the year that he held this office he consorted with persons such as José Lins do Rêgo and Rachel de Queiroz, forming some lasting friendships, and was considered the head of the group of Northeastern writers becoming so well known. Now remarried, with friends and recognition, Graciliano found life more satisfying.

At the end of a year he had left his post to accept that of Director of Public Instruction in Alagoas and was back in Palmeira dos Indios. Using one of his earlier short novels, *A carta* (The Letter), as a point of departure, in 1932 Graciliano began the composition of *São Bernardo* which, despite the interruption of a serious illness, he completed in rather short order. This was a period of relatively great literary productivity for Graciliano. Nineteen thirty-three saw not only the publication of *São Bernardo*. The novelist began *Angústia*, which was based on the other of his short novels, *Entre grades* (Between Bars); the last chapter of *Angústia* was written in a single evening. *São Bernardo* appeared in 1934, *Angústia* in 1936.

Significantly, Graciliano's first three novels are written in the first person. *Vidas Sêcas* is not, but the writer has penetrated his characters so thoroughly that, despite the use of the third person, the reader scarcely notices that it is not the first person. In *Infância* and *Memórias do Cárcere* Graciliano resumes the use of the first person

— to be sure, the first work has many autobiographical elements and the second is pure autobiography. Seldom can an author disengage himself from one of his leading characters, and, as he himself seems to have realized, Graciliano less than most.

One always assumes that the writer is hiding behind the narrator-character, although this device does not necessarily serve as a mask. In Graciliano's case the assumption is quite correct, especially as regards the identity of philosophies of life and art between characters and author, and their awareness of them. Graciliano's world is seemingly one in which Naturalistic determinism reigns largely un-opposed, and in which people suffer with few amenities or poetry of any sort. Like their author, his characters are, however, very con-scious and critical of themselves. Their surroundings tend to be accessory, other people secondary, and any effort at satisfaction or a higher emotion illusory. It is as though man wished to be nature's ac-complice, but ennobling himself through consciousness as he is destroyed. Thus, Graciliano's style is quite different from that of Machado de Assis, whose narrator, Dom Casmurro, uses precise composition and language in an attempt to deceive himself and his reader. Graciliano's narrators are careful with language, sometimes to the point of contradicting their station in life thereby, but in the in-terest of revealing the truth about themselves and their fellows as directly as possible. Like their creator, they employ honest, earthy language when required by the subject. In a sense they are "cultivated backlanders," to use the epithet that came to be applied to Graciliano both as a writer and as a man. The semi-legendary figure thus described becomes all the more vivid when concrete com-parisons are made between him and his chief characters. Whether or not they are autobiographical, whether or not Graciliano was proud of his work, they reveal their creator's personality. Their world, although it reflects his faithfully, is one in which Graciliano could ac-commodate himself better than in his own.

It has been noted that the study of literature and writing became a refuge early in the life of Graciliano Ramos. His background and en-vironment prepared him to be not only withdrawn but misanthropic. Although he had written and published poetry, Graciliano's most im-portant works exhibit little that is normally thought of as poetic im-agination, aesthetic beauty, or gentle emotion. These seem to have slight place in the grimly realistic world of the author and the man.

João Valério, the protagonist of *Caetés,* seeks to forget his hum-drum existence, including what turns out to be a petty love affair, in the novel that he vainly attempts to compose. Paulo Honório and Luís da Silva wish to re-create and understand their tragic lives. *São Bernardo* is Paulo Honórios's memoirs and *Angústia* the narrative of Luís da Silva's derangement. As João Valério observes and meditates more than he acts, he realizes that true life closely resembles the book on the life of cannibals that he is trying to create with such difficulty, so much so that he no longer feels the need to write it. *Caetés* is that book. Paulo Honório sets out consciously and conscientiously to order what remains of his life by ordering and setting down his recollections of what has happened. Emotion seems occasionally to impede his efforts, and he fuses periods in time and events. Luís da Silva's unbalanced mind interferes constantly with his narration. The author and reader collaborate with each other and with the characters to establish the necessary relationships and draw conclusions. Reality is thus transformed into art, which gives form and meaning to life. What makes the process unique in Graciliano's novels, as well as in the autobiographical writing, is his deliberateness and the degree to which the results are personal.

Apparently quite different from other works because of its division into units resembling short stories more than the chapters of a novel, the use of the third person, and the more humble station of its principal characters, *Vidas Sêcas* is as representative of Graciliano as an artist and a man as his other writings. Although not his most successful genre, the short story was practiced by Graciliano to a considerable degree. Apart from collections of writings designated as short stories, there is evidence of his inclination toward the genre in the structure of *Infância* and *Memórias do Cárcere* as well as in *Vidas Sêcas*. As to the third person, it has already been noted that this device does not prevent the reader from imagining often that the characters, who address themselves in the third person, are in fact using the first. The supposedly objective device was no doubt required because of the extremely primitive nature in every respect of Fabiano, his family, and their dog. Yet these *sertanejos* are types with whom Graciliano was most familiar and could identify; they represent him especially well when they reveal surprising depths of intellect and emotion, despite their seeming incapacity to communicate verbally.

A Modernist in spite of himself, Graciliano, whether he makes use of a narrator or not, or narrates in his own first person, plunges the reader into the matter of his work. There is generally no pretense of having planned the book in advance; on the contrary, more often there is a protest against such planning or a complaint of inability to plan. Largely memoirs and episodic in character, Graciliano's works have less obvious need of structure than other forms of literature. Paulo Honório had engaged *littérateurs* of his acquaintance to write his story, but soon became disgusted with their artifices. These were no doubt attributable as much to their traditionalist rhetoric as to the composite nature of the project. (Incidentally, it is interesting that Graciliano should later have collaborated with several Northeastern colleagues in a similar venture or misadventure.) Paulo Honório chooses to tell his own tale forthrightly, with a minimum of false literature. It will be recalled that João Valério concludes that the book he has been struggling to produce is vain compared with life as he observes it and meditates upon it. Luís da Silva, despite apparent good taste and a keen critical faculty, is a hack writer who thinks vaguely of composing a great work one day. Much like João Valério's description and commentary, Luís' narrative of his background and recent tragic events turns out to be the book that he would probably never have written. *Vidas Sêcas* is a similar record of the innermost thoughts and feelings of Fabiano and those close to him, kept by Graciliano without benefit of a narrator. He had always dealt quite faithfully in real life, if not precisely in autobiography, and did not therefore need the intermediary of a narrator-character to lend plausibility to his work. The autobiographies do not, of course, require this particular literary device either, although they are not lacking in others.

As long as he wrote about the kind of people he knew intimately (and chiefly about himself), the lives they led, the problems they faced, great or small, and the setting in which they resolved them, Graciliano seems to have felt that his stories should for the most part tell themselves. There was much less laissez-faire, however, in his attitude regarding content and style. His function was to provide the knowledge necessary to the reader and to analyze it, sometimes openly, sometimes more discreetly, but always in language that was as pure, clear, and honest as he could make it. Graciliano and his characters, whether they write or not, are sociologists and psychologists in their fields, and both realists and classicists, if not with respect to overall form, certainly in regard to particulars. Theirs are reactions and accommodations to the life of their day and art, past and present, as well as reflections of personal temperament. Purity and clarity of style were difficult to find in most traditional and contemporary Brazilian literature, and Modernist honesty seemed of little value to Graciliano if expressed in gross, obscure language. If others had been able to add color and relevance for their times to classical forms, so could he, and *le mot juste* could be a well-placed regionalism or earthy expression and remain respectable. Graciliano disciplined himself to these ends.

As to the gentler emotions, their background and temperament tend to make Graciliano and his protagonists repress them. The misanthropes among them resemble other misanthropes, however, and the rougher types are no more of one piece than they. Both kinds of characters require and respond to love, although their awareness of this need may become clear only after they have been subjected to and purged by more violent emotions. Paulo Honório's case at the conclusion of *São Bernardo* is very representative of Graciliano's experience and philosophy:

> Four chapters constitute an epilogue within the narrative. Paulo Honório is grief-stricken in his restrained manner. When Seu Ribeiro and Dona Glória desert him, he treats them according to Madalena's last requests. But political and consequent disasters now befall him too. In the final chapter, a true epilogue to the reader, Paulo Honório is faced with complete destruction. He summarizes and meditates on his life in all its aspects and concludes that it is entirely futile. Yet if Paulo Honório's story has been followed with a maximum of objectivity, as it seems both author and narrator have intended, one must find his punishment exaggeratedly severe: on one level, society's fault is enormous; on the other, fate seems to have taken a hand. If Madalena appears less guilty it is because Paulo Honório, on whom these forces have had longer to work, overshadows her in every way. Both have paid for their sins, but Paulo Honório continues to pay. It may be, too, that Fortune does not spin her wheel completely at random.
>
> As Paulo Honório suffers, he learns. Perhaps with greater understanding will come also greater identification for and sympathy with his bestialized fellows, for he is again approaching their economic and therefore social level. Although Paulo Honório says that he has no love for his son, it has been noted that he intends to be a good father to him. And Madalena's memory, a fond one, is constantly before him. Paulo Honório's pessimistic observations are undoubtedly true with respect to the past, but love purified by tragedy may be conditioning him anew. For what other reason would Madalena's memory be virtually unstained for him now? In any case, if he and the reader of his narrative have learned any moral lesson, Paulo Honório's life and *São Bernardo* have not been in vain.[3]

These words of mine take on a fuller meaning when they are applied to the author's life prior to the appearance of *São Bernardo*. They are especially significant when considered in the light of what was to happen to Graciliano after 1934.

In 1936, while still Director of Public Instruction in Alagoas, Graciliano Ramos was suddenly arrested in Maceió, apparently for political reasons. Transferred first to Recife, then to Rio de Janeiro, in the hold of a ship with other prisoners, both ordinary and political, he was to spend a year in several correctional institutions in the capital without being tried. Ironically, although presumed a Communist, he did not join the Party until 1945. He was released in 1937, his already poor health quite broken. Graciliano's fame, if not his fortune, as a novelist and writer of short stories was considerable, however. This time he would not leave Rio to return to the Northeast. He received a number of honors, was appointed Inspector of Secondary Education, and continued to be active as a writer, as the chronology reveals.

I have had occasion to discuss *Infância* (1945) as an artistic presentation in short, loosely related units somewhat resembling short stories, of Graciliano's earliest years. *Vidas Sêcas* (1938), which is almost in short-story form too, in some respects foreshadows *Infância* in content and form, as well as other works written after Graciliano's release from prison. A number of the narratives in *Insônia* (Insomnia) [1947], whether in the first or third person, are equally autobiographical. Some reflect his childhood, others his illness and hospital experience before he was incarcerated, and a few became part of the posthumous *Memórias do Cárcere* (1953). These memoirs of course deal with the period of the author's imprisonment, but reflect also other times in his life. All of Graciliano's work is a repetition with variants of his whole existence. As he constantly revised a given work because of dissatisfaction and the desire to be perfect, so from work to work he reevaluated his life and career from fresh, complementary points of view.

In *Memórias do Cárcere* Graciliano Ramos reveals the worst and the best of his experience as an adult. He has been forced almost without respite to come to grips with all forms of humanity while in prison. Like his protagonists, he has been unable frequently to escape mental and physical anguish except through the most primitive forms of sedation and apathy. His attitudes toward his fellows and the human condition are reinforced, to be sure, and, on those occasions when he is able to work, he is more than normally convinced of the futility of writing. Yet Graciliano is sometimes surprised, perhaps all the more so at the time of composition, after a lapse of some years, to observe the kindness of individuals and solidarity of certain groups of his recent acquaintance.

It is almost as though the note of hope to be found in earlier works were wishful thinking on his part, now realized in fact as he recollects, and doubtless reinterprets, life in prison after the fact. Graciliano wonders if his memory fails him and if the reader will believe what he writes of good works performed under abnormal conditions. Accustomed as he is to contrary actions and to considering these universal, he further wonders if he is capable of being less hostile, more outgoing, and truly generous. Much like Paulo Honório, Graciliano finds it hard to believe people completely selfless. Like Paulo Honório, too, he regrets his objectivity and consequent pessimism. This regret, plus some good deeds, save him and his protagonists after João Valério from the cynicism and pettiness of Machado de Assis' narrators. One admires Graciliano for his powers of observation and urgent need for the most part to record what he sees and thinks as impartially as possible.[4] Again resembling his protagonists, the novelist-memorialist considers the material, psychological, and moral problems of life chiefly from his own experience, leaving little to the imagination either in the realm of nonfiction or fiction.

CHAPTER 2

The Sociologist-Psychologist

A T the time of the events of the Semana de Arte Moderna in São Paulo (1922), Graciliano Ramos was a shopkeeper and sometime *littérateur* in Palmeira dos Indios. The sonnets and short stories that he had written gave little evidence that Graciliano would be hailed as a Modernist and even as a leader of the Modernist novelists of the Northeast. His voracious reading of nineteenth-century European and Brazilian novelists prepared him to be quite traditional in form and style. Yet the training that he underwent by studying classic and essentially classical authors included the application of their realism to his own reality. Witness his famous reports of 1929 - 1930 to the Governor of Alagoas. Graciliano's newspaper work kept him abreast of current developments in all spheres. He was aware of the defects of Modernism, but also of the advantages that some accommodation with it could bring him, artistically and perhaps in a practical sense as well. Before he was discovered by the Modernists, however, through the publicity received by his reports on conditions in Palmeira dos Indios, Gilberto Freyre's well-known promulgation of Regionalism took place in Recife (1926). Freyre's intention was not to reaffirm the description of picturesque landscapes and quaint customs typical of the old regionalism, but to develop a new science on sound scientific bases, chiefly sociological, both for the intrinsic value of such study and to counteract the often chaotic and obscure Modernism of São Paulo.

Much of what is significant in modern Brazilian thought dates from the initiation of Freyre's major studies, particularly in his part of the Brazilian Northeast. *Casa Grande e Senzala* (1933), soon followed by other essays in a series, have become classics not only in Brazil but throughout the world. Their author is recognized as a major creative scholar and thinker — sociologist, social historian,

[33]

anthropologist, and social psychologist — as well as a man of letters. Revolutionary in content and methodology, Freyre is not so removed from the Modernists as he gave people to believe. He is more conservative in sociopolitical attitudes, and especially in literary tastes, than many of his followers in the Northeast. His wish seemed to be to continue the traditional rivalry between São Paulo and the older parts of the country, with leadership to remain in the latter's hands. Freyre has reviewed the Brazilian past in its every aspect and detail and caused others, whether they agree with him completely or not, to trace the evolution of Brazilian culture. Moreover, its beginnings in the patriarchal family, Indian and Negro slavery, and a single-crop economy are repeated elsewhere in Brazil and in Latin America generally. Throughout its history Brazil has been a unique blend of many, equally important elements in a primarily tropical setting. What makes the country what it is today are people of many races, creeds, and languages become more or less homogeneous through a certain process of democratization. It must be underscored that Freyre's chief distinctions are greater pragmatism than the Modernists in the matter at hand, fundamentally a reevaluation of Brazilian culture, and greater rationalism in thought and mode of expression than they or his fellow Regionalists.

Despite his isolation and dissatisfaction with his work, it should have been somewhat gratifying to Graciliano Ramos to learn that *Caetés,* completed by 1926, corresponded in part to the tenets of Regionalism. Although this novel was patterned largely after the works of writers like Flaubert and Eça de Queiroz, Graciliano had applied their lessons to a Brazilian subject. Further, he had learned something of the use of language from Brazilian masters of prose, some of whom had applied the same lessons from Europe. Whether or not it was a source of satisfaction to Graciliano, *Caetés* and *Casa Grande e Senzala* appeared in the same year (1933). All of the creators of the new novel of the Brazilian Northeast had preceded them in publication, the precursor José Américo de Almeida by five years *(A Bagaceira, 1928)* and Rachel de Queiroz by three *(O Quinze,* 1930, and *João Miguel,* 1931). Preceding him by one year, Lins do Rêgo mourned the passing of the patriarchal system *(Menino de Engenho,* 1932), and Jorge Amado *(Pais do Carnaval,* 1932, and *Cacau,* 1933) denounced the old system and the new. Freyre described the feudal agrarian society with relative objectivity and prepared to trace its partial transformation in urban conditions *(Sobrados e Mocambos* [The Mansions and the Shanties], 1936).

Prompted by sadness and bitterness analogous to the sentiments of Lins do Rêgo and Amado, but also by a desire to understand and correct, Graciliano first exercised his talents in a satire of society in Palmeira dos Indios. Following a reverse chronology, he was to describe and comment on the urban and rural life of other places where he lived, always emphasizing the pragmatic and the rational.

Although Graciliano does not dwell on the landscape for its own sake as had and did other Regionalists, which he sometimes felt to be a lack, his impressionistic style in the manner of the Goncourt brothers and Eça de Queiroz does not exclude landscape. It is there to orient the reader with regard to the action, and the characters and reader concerning the sociopsychological meaning of the action. For landscape is more than mere description; it is the result of one's vision of the surroundings and may be transformed depending on points of view. Not only are there changes of perspective physically, as an individual changes position or as the action moves from individual to individual, but there are transformations as a given group or character views his surroundings differently. Paulo Honório thought of São Bernardo, as of everything and everyone about him, as an instrument to greater wealth and power. Later he begins to see unexpected beauty in the *fazenda*. Gradually, his contemplation of the place and meditations on the meaning of his actions will provide him with a more complete picture of life.

This kind of personal landscape is almost absent in *Caetés*. More typical is the frequent use of objective references by the narrator to Palmeira dos Indios as a place and a presence and stylized descriptions of its inhabitants. If the reader is not familiar with the provincial city he soon becomes so through repetition, much as Graciliano did after many years of residence there. Like the long-time resident, the reader does not as a rule see or need to see the places that he visits regularly. Exceptionally, some special physical or emotional condition causes João Valério's attention to be drawn briefly to some aspect of the environment. The scene is then likely to be deformed impressionistically as under a spotlight rather than illuminated in detail as with the microscope. At times the narrator-character focuses more objectively on a scene to provide ironic contrast with his situation. Frequent are the allusions to several distinctive sounds of the city, which are most effective in making its presence felt in somewhat mysterious and even ominous fashion. In any case, with all of Graciliano's experimentation there is greater sociopsychological truth than with more conventional Realism.

A genuine landscape in the subjective, Romantic sense of fusion of man with nature, each having equally active roles, is found only once in *Caetés*. Comparing himself with Barroca, a local politician and great orator, João Valério is dissatisfied with his lack of success. As he awaits the procession and Luísa's arrival, twilight falls and he sadly contemplates the land. João Valério feels that he is a plateau surrounded by obstacles like the mountains that he sees on all sides. Immediately, however, he returns to the sociological view of Palmeira dos Indios and the customary enumeration of landmarks. Later, after Adrião's death and the end of the affair between João Valério and Luísa, the narrator again retraces his steps. The places are the same, and his memories of what he once felt for nature because of his passion are clear; but his feelings are different, leaving him indifferent to the beauty that he now recollects. Like João Valério or his colleagues of the group of Northeastern writers, Graciliano could be a master of true landscape. Unlike Lins do Rêgo or Jorge Amado, however, he preferred to exercise this art sparingly. More of a classicist, he employed local color primarily as a backdrop for his gallery of regional types or his study of protagonists psychologically like himself.

In *Caetés*, then, the city of Palmeira dos Indios plays an important role as the setting of the action, such as it is. More important, the city is the setting in which Graciliano presents representatives of the upper and lower middle classes that he knew so well there. He did not think any better of these people than does the narrator through whose somewhat picaresque comings and goings he presents them. The view of Palmeira dos Indios and commentary on its inhabitants that he gives the reader become a satirical chronicle of the place with João Valério's story merely constituting one rather minor episode in the context of the whole. Sociological types are created from Graciliano's observations and selection of salient features by which to characterize them. In the tradition of some of the greatest European social realism, the author does not develop secondary characters; indeed, principal ones remain relatively static. They are described and behave always in much the same way, so that they become rather predictable. The author or narrator, and eventually the reader, function as puppeteers superior to tic-ridden caricatures of human beings. Like Balzac, Graciliano may have considered himself the secretary of his society, but he permitted himself a good deal of editorializing in the minutes.

As the title of the novel indicates and João Valério explains, the

Caeté Indians were the former inhabitants of Palmeira dos Indios and they were cannibals. The present-day residents — although the victims among them may be tragic or at least pathetic — are just as vicious in their way. The notary, the priest, the pharmacist, all of them lack intellectual curiosity and serious purpose, mechanically following humdrum routines in the same old places at the same old times. To avoid engulfment by the dullness of the boardinghouse, the newspaper office, and the homes of notables where they gather periodically, they vary interminable discussions of daily concerns by discussing equally monotonous petty gossip such as the affair between Luísa and João Valério. Except for the latter, they do not seem to perceive that, as they tear and are torn apart, the monster that they have created that is their culture is swallowing them up. The city of Palmeira dos Indios that summarizes the several parts of the environment and symbolizes it as a separate presence, largely unseen but familiar through place-names and especially sounds, engulfs them.

São Bernardo is the memoirs of the protagonist, and virtually all the action therefore takes place in the past. Like Machado de Assis' famous narrators, although not always to the same ends, Paulo Honório knows what he must set down and arranges the material to suit himself. Along with a certain compulsion to think things out clearly, there is some pure distraction that is part of the therapy as well. Included in order to situate or enhance the action is a considerable amount of landscape. Despite the increased quantity, however, every detail is carefully selected and integrated because it is felt to be necessary. Paulo Honório goes so far as to say that he does not describe certain things because they are superfluous or will become apparent of their own accord. Indeed, by means of very short descriptions interspersing or accompanying narration, the reader gradually becomes well acquainted with the *fazenda,* much as he grew familiar with Palmeira dos Indios during the course of João Valério's walks. That there are more variety and color in the details given in São Bernardo bespeaks greater interest in both author and narrator. As Paulo Honório recollects with tragic irony the events that brought him to the present situation, he attempts successfully to recapture the past, simultaneously rejecting a part of it in order to recoup another part of his loss. More contact with people like Madalena and experience with suffering will bring increased success.

Like Graciliano, Paulo Honório is gifted with great powers of observation and a keen artistic sense. At his worst as a human being, when he thinks with pride of the *fazenda* and wealth so ruthlessly but laboriously acquired, he has a certain tenderness for the place and the living beings on it. His descriptions contain elements of animate and inanimate nature, and one follows without being told in so many words the progress made by the master of São Bernardo in restoring the property and making it flourish. Purely ornamental scenes begin to rival those of fat cattle grazing in green fields and new roofs shining next to lush forests when Madalena enters Paulo Honório's life. The memorialist now perceives flowers. The stream thinks itself a river and sings after the storm. The waterfall is adorned with foam. Descriptions of the color, sound, and movement about him as integral parts of his story continue to interest the narrator after his wife's suicide. Now, however, the elements in the landscape that represent material wealth grow small and unreal. The cattle are celluloid toys and the woodcutters mere figurines from Paulo Honório's observation post in the church tower and the vantage point of his new objectivity. Nature for its own sake continues to gain his appreciation, which tells the reader as much about Paulo Honório as about the beauty of nature.

The city is of no immediate consequence in São Bernardo, and there is no collectivity composed of social classes for the author or narrator to deal with. Emphasis is placed on characters as individuals rather than as representatives of groups in society. Virtually all the action takes place on the *fazenda,* with the background necessary to understand Paulo Honório, before he acquired it, worked in in the customary economical manner. It has already been noted that there is more landscape in this novel than in *Caetés.* On the surface one should expect this, given the locale of *São Bernardo.* Yet *Caetés,* generally classified as a Naturalistic work because of certain aspects of content and style, might well have greater explicit description of the environment. The fact is that *São Bernardo* is more seriously Naturalistic in basic philosophy, especially in Paulo Honório's rather picaresque antecedents and behavior in acquiring his empire, as well as more psychological in character development.

The techniques used in *São Bernardo,* which do not vary as much as the content and sentiments, may best be characterized as classical-realistic. For it must be remembered that they are practiced always by the same person, a narrator who in the present is seeking to recollect, order, and understand his past with a view to surviving in the future. He conveys the recent period of emotion, both elated and disturbed, in the same laconic style as the one used before he was touched by the passions of love; the only new feature of how he writes is repetition in different contexts of what has affected him. Despite Paulo Honório's guilt and that of other individuals, the reader feels that the environment, society, nature, or fate is more to blame. The perspective, however, is that of an authentic individual of tragic-heroic proportions. In *Caetés* the protagonist is scarcely distinguishable from and shares equally in guilt with his fellows in the petty world of Palmeira dos Indios.

Despite the similarities that link the narrators of *Caetés, São Bernardo,* and *Angústia* and their goals in telling their stories, Luís da Silva is quite different from João Valério and Paulo Honório. In the long, seldom interrupted interior monologue that is *Angústia,* Luís' deranged mind confuses memories of the several phases of his life and places in which he has lived. As detached as he is normally, there is no reason why João Valério should not record what he sees, hears, and thinks in orderly fashion. Even Paulo Honório's most painful recollections are presented quite rationally. The weak scion of a degenerating *sertanejo* line and culture, Luís is overwhelmed also by urban life in Maceió. He is the product of his heredity and environment, the perfect victim of Naturalism and Freudian symbolism, until he turns destruction into salvation by an act that is both mad and heroic. Only at the end of his story does Luís realize that this is the beginning. The reader, too, clearly perceives what has happened, as well as a circular pattern characteristic of form and content in Graciliano's works.

The exterior action of *Angústia* unfolds in many sordid parts of Maceió, but Luís' descriptions, much as in the case of João Valério, are scarcely more than allusions. Less through the author's experimentation or the narrator's caprice, Luís sometimes focuses on physical elements that affect him psychologically and morally: grease, decay, violence, and, finally, sex. He is much concerned with water and cleaning himself. This is true whether it is his immediate surroundings that preoccupy him or associations with other places and times which they lead him to make. These spatial-temporal parallels occur frequently, with no apparent desire of his to escape to the *sertão,* despite the traditional longing of natives always to return; for Luís finds nothing in that barren region to improve his present environment. Grimy bars and filthy goat pens are equated, and he has no worse fate in Maceió than his father or grandfather in their dirty hammocks or stained shrouds. Luís is most absorbed in his own limited world, rejected and rejecting à la Roquentin of Sartre's

Nausée (Nausea). For the master of São Bernardo it is the world of a large *fazenda,* always dynamic and full of color whatever his attitude may be. For Luís it is the miserable boardinghouse in which he lives, especially the garbage-strewn courtyard where he meets Marina. The whole is static and repugnant objectively, but also because Luís is an outwardly passive, generally depressed man. He sees everything in shadow or haze. The only action that he observes, apart from that of rats, is of persons leading lives for the most part as gray as his. These include Seu Ramalho and Dona Adélia, Marina's parents, and eventually Marina herself, all victimized by society and its ills. Urban dweller or backlander, it makes little difference. Luís is physically and emotionally stifled by his environment, as João Valério is stifled intellectually and morally by his.

Uncertain, anguished to the end, fearing that the man who symbolizes all his frustrations will escape in the fog while he decides whether or not to kill him, Luís resembles Graciliano. Like Graciliano, who, assisted by cigarettes and brandy, abandoned his customary mode of work to write the conclusion of *Angústia* in one feverish night, Luís finally murders Julião Tavares under the impulse of his madness. After a long convalescence, which is his punishment for the crime and constitutes a good part of the narrative, Luís is cured of all disgust and purged of all guilt. Similarly, Graciliano seems to have been relieved of some of his problems as a man and an artist by his suffering in prison. Much as a patient recounts his life to his psychiatrist, Luís relates his bitter childhood, his deprived adolescence, and his humiliating youth, all phases intimately experienced by Graciliano and the reader of his works.

Befitting the region of the *sêca* (drought), such landscape as can be found in *Vidas Sêcas* is dazzling in brilliant sunlight rather than dimmed by fog. Colors are vivid in the cruel glare: the monotonous yellow of the *catinga* (scrub vegetation), the ominous black of the vultures, and the relentless blue of the sky, so bright that to look at it brings tears. The flood of light is as devastating as rain might be elsewhere, and is here also at times, physically, emotionally, artistically. When it is focused, sparingly as are all of Graciliano's devices, it illuminates both cause and effect. Scenes of destruction are captured briefly by the bold touch of an impressionist who knows which traits to seize upon and repeat with variations in order to suggest and fix the tragedy. Even more than from what the author describes or the characters see, the reader learns of the climate or changes in season by their effect on the way of life and preoccupations of the protagonists. As the title indicates, more than one life is treated in this work, and the life of Fabiano's family represents and symbolizes that of the majority of *sertanejos* who lead parched, barren, and silent lives.

Even in times of relative plenty, the characters recall with fear the implacable cycle of the seasons; always they suffer the socioeconomic ills of a society influenced in large part by its regional environment. Their view of things in town (Buíque), despite the added strangeness of the surroundings, does not differ greatly from their reactions at home. Fabiano's dream of security on the *fazenda* is shattered, as he knew it must be, by the next drought. Vitória probably realized that her dream of comfort and social status in the form of a leather bed would be destroyed by the landlord's customary cheating. A rare note of triumph is sounded when Fabiano, despite his many virtues, behaves more nobly with the "yellow soldier" who brutalized him in the city than could be anticipated:

In the third chapter from the end, "O Soldado Amarelo," Fabiano again encounters the soldier, this time out in the *catinga,* and almost kills him, instinctively, as a natural enemy. He stops himself when he sees a man before him. When he recognizes him as the man who insulted him, Fabiano experiences an intensely dramatic inner conflict: avenge his honor by striking down this cringing wretch, or be a decadent coward by letting him go? In the interior monologue he achieves revenge, vicariously as it were, as well as purification of all flaws, real or imagined, so that he emerges from the struggle triumphant, justified, and magnanimous. The about-face at the end of the encounter is external and does not diminish Fabiano, as may his enforced humility in scenes with the *patrão* [boss] and other symbols of social injustice. The soldier is so weak and Fabiano so strong in the *catinga* that the latter's generosity is the impressive quality.

Out of his element, Fabiano manages to be quite tragic by his occasional open and frequent mental rebellion. But no one expects him to be truly heroic on a level where, through ignorance and impotence, he must interpret economic forces as immutable destiny in order to survive. When there is nothing more to lose, Fabiano's primitive nature, credulous and bordering on madness, engages him in a battle to protect his water supply against flocks of birds migrating from the *sêca.* Magnificently heroic but necessarily futile, this scene is followed by cruel demoralization, feelings of guilt, and a need to flee.[1]

In fact, Graciliano may have made Fabiano nobler than is entirely plausible, more in keeping with his own evolution and that of his other protagonists. João Valério causes Luísa's husband to kill himself and views the matter and its consequences indifferently as another episode in the cannibalistic history of society. Paulo Honório contributes to Madalena's suicide and Luís da Silva kills Julião. Both are conditioned to commit their crimes, but also determined by love, suffering, and somewhat more of a moral code than João Valério possessed to feel remorse and emerge healthier, better men. Noble savage that he is, Fabiano is purer in the first instance, without the benefit of idyllic nature. He is further purified by the harsh socioeconomic conditions under which he and his family must survive. The romantic, dramatic extremes needed to convert João Valério's relatively sophisticated successors from cynicism or apathy were not required in Fabiano's case.

Infância (1945) is close to *Vidas Sêcas* (1938) in that it records much of his early experience already transformed by the adult Graciliano in the latter work as well as in the other novels and in short stories. It does not, of course, recapture the completely direct, frank realism of the reports of the Prefect of Palmeira dos Indios. Nor does it yet have the authenticity and depth of the *Memórias do Cárcere* (1954). Presented are stylized recollections as a child might narrate them of the author's most vivid childhood impressions of family, regions and towns in which they lived, and different aspects of the harsh land and crude society. Graciliano's memories of the education that he received in piecemeal fashion, for the most part under stern taskmasters, are of great significance. Equally important are disappointments experienced in Rio when he went there to try his luck among newspapermen and *littérateurs* of the day, as well as the initial condescendence, followed by surprised admiration, showed him by these types when they later visited him in his provincial home. Episodes from *Infância* and anecdotes concerning his youth and early maturity, generally found in other remarks by Graciliano or friends and critics of his, help the reader to interpret more fully Graciliano's vision of life and art.

Most interesting are the *Memórias* which, although *of* Graciliano's imprisonment and the world he discovered during it, are also *from* prison. As in other works, and for similar reasons of physical suffering, emotional anguish, or mental confusion requiring therapy, the protagonist often associates different periods and places in his life. The years elapsed between his release and the time of writing is another factor that both increases and hampers the memorialist's objectivity. On the nightmarish trip from Recife to Rio de Janeiro in the crowded, stinking hold of a ship, with stops at Maceió, Bahia, and finally Rio, he has occasion to recall the voyage to the capital made in his youth. The sights and especially the people encountered in 1914, although subject to his usual misanthropy, are nevertheless in considerable contrast to those of 1936. Meeting representatives from all parts of Brazil and all walks of life, Graciliano selects salient features of theirs as types and individuals to emphasize, much as he creates characters impressionistically in his novels. Some of the criminal and political prisoners are subjects in the short stories of *Insônia* (1947), developed in situations that must have been theirs prior to their imprisonment.

Above all Graciliano analyzes their actions and, as he does so, realizes that people do not always correspond to the understanding of humanity that he had on the outside. Perhaps exceptionally bad circumstances do determine behavior for the better as well as for the worse. Good works are performed gratuitously, it seems, sometimes by the most sordid individuals under the most sordid conditions. The novelist imagined such generosity for some of his protagonists without quite believing it possible. As for lesser characters at whose hands these might suffer, they are usually considered mere instruments of some superior force. Graciliano himself does not blame his wrongdoers as much as the government or the system; but that they are mere instruments does not absolve them entirely or make them good. When Graciliano witnesses magnanimity in real life, he finds it difficult to accept that truth can be stranger than fiction (although he does not make the comparisons that I do). Graciliano especially wonders if he is capable of such behavior. In his pain and remembrances of pain, he appears sometimes to be more a philosopher, clinging to Naturalistic pessimism, than a sociologist or psychologist. Always he is an artist, however deprecating of his work and person, with an inner compulsion to keep writing.

CHAPTER 3

The Artist-Philosopher[1]

I Caetés

WHEN *Caetés* appeared in 1933, it was noted to be different from the Regionalist literature then emerging in the Northeast in sociology and art. For one thing, the novelists who had already made their debut in that part of the country revealed the excesses of most reformers, including some that were characteristic of the Modernists of São Paulo. The most objective of the new writers of Northeastern Brazil, Jorge Amado, had nevertheless made a pro-proletariat tract of *Cacau*, romantically proclaiming the sentiment of the people against the capitalist class and the liberty of the writer to use crude language. All members of the group were purported to be Realists or Naturalists, but "documents" of lower-class life and protests against social and political injustice did not disguise their basic Romanticism. Lins do Rêgo was less political than Amado, and Rachel de Queiroz more restrained in language; yet both exhibited a certain sentimentality and superficiality with regard to the people they depicted. Graciliano too was concerned with the Northeast and solutions for its problems, but also with the form, techniques, and language of the novel. A true Realist as well as a Classicist, he poured Brazilian language into traditional Portuguese molds. Further, he portrayed Brazilian reality through the eyes of protagonists who were both Brazilian and universally human.

At first glance *Caetés* is merely a very good example of the type of novel developed by the Northeastern group. Its excellence may be explained by the work already produced in the Northeast or, better, by Graciliano's age and preparation when he wrote it in 1925 - 1928. It is a direct attack against society, expressed in colloquial Brazilian Portuguese, well written to be sure, in an apparently objective narrative following the linear pattern established since the beginnings of the novel. Whether great or mediocre, writers old and new found it easy to number chapters consecutively and tell their stories in more or less chronological order, either in the third person of the omniscient author or in the first person of a narrator. The use of a narrator is somewhat more delicate, for he must be a character in his own right in order to prevent the author from taking over at the same time that he exhibits the qualities required to tell a good story. Here, again, Graciliano uses a conventional device, making his narrator a would-be novelist, except that the latter eventually abandons the work that he was writing in favor of the narrative that turns out to be *Caetés*.

This variation is significant in providing an instrument of irony by which João Valério can measure himself and his society against the Indians who are his subject. As he considers his savage behavior in several instances and that of Palmeira dos Indios, which has destroyed all but some artifacts and a few human relics of that other society, he realizes that the Indians' barbarism symbolizes that of the moderns. Whereas João Valério found himself too ignorant to study the Caetés as a social scientist, the psychological parallel becomes most clear to him whether from an individual or a social point of view. Meanwhile, the world of the primitive Indians, doubtless somewhat idyllic because of his ignorance, is an occasional refuge for João Valério.

Finally, not because he learns more about it factually, but because he cannot keep his world distinct from that of the cannibals, João Valério renounces the project. It is not, as in much modern literature, that the past is interpreted in terms of the present, but the reverse, which is perhaps more typical of conventional thinking in real life. Apart from the tracing of origins, history can be utilized in regional literature to create or destroy the myths of a people, depending on the goals of the author. History may be the device of escapist literature, or a means of sharpening analogies between the past and the present. João Valério is not the writer of modern epic literature who objectivizes figures from the past so that they may judge themselves and be judged; rather, he judges his fellows in terms of the cannibals, and posterity comes off no better than in real life. Although he is little the wiser about the Caetés, João Valério is confirmed in his understanding of himself and his contemporaries.

In the satire that includes the protagonist as well as the society of Palmeira dos Indios, Graciliano creates the opportunity for João Valério to have his own dimension as a character. Otherwise, the narrator and author would be one, and the advantage of the first-person "eyewitness" would be lost. João Valério has this opportunity whenever he meditates on the subject of his book, but also on other occasions as he reviews different thoughts and emotions by himself. The direct monologue is used sparingly, however, for the narrator is less inclined to introspection than to presenting a view of society. Descriptions that are much the same as those of an omniscient third person or dialogues where characters speak independently give this view. The reader's conclusions are that the individual and his society scarcely differ, and that as a consequence man lives as though alone in a group of people as solitary as he, equally unknown and unknowing. Something of a Sartrean hero ahead of his time, João Valério might well say, "L'enfer, c'est les autres." In considering the ending of the work, one may suspect that Graciliano was not interested in pursuing a petty love affair of limited social interest. On the other hand, it is possible also to give the conclusion an Existentialist interpretation, or even one that recalls Madame de La Fayette's famous novel.[2]

Except for Luísa, the characters of *Caetés* are developed as types representative of the society of Palmeira dos Indios. That Luísa is scarcely developed at all does not imply any special delicacy on Graciliano's part concerning women, for there are feminine counterparts of the male prototypes in *Caetés*, nor that he wishes to envelop her in mystery with a view to writing a more exciting love story. The affair between João Valério and Luísa is of little significance compared to the satire of provincial society in this work. Having no interest in a love affair as such, nor certainly any wish to exploit it sentimentally, Graciliano nevertheless pays sufficient attention to the psychology of João Valério to make him adequate as his narrator and spokesman regarding Palmeira dos Indios. His desire to possess Luísa forms part of the narrator's motivation to comment on society, but only a part. Several other ambitions motivate him, contradictory and confusing despite some success, until he reaches his pessimistic conclusion. Like João Valério, who is experimenting with life, Graciliano experiments with art. Like his protagonist, too, he enjoys a degree of success, revealing characteristics that he will utilize more completely in later volumes: João Valério is already the creation of the environment, as are his fellows, but also its creator. Despite this promise of what his major works will be, Graciliano is bewildered, if not as a philosopher of pessimism, as a novelist. Love becomes a prime mover in his other novels. Had he developed the love of Luísa and João Valério more fully, in line with other aspects of this protagonist, *Caetés* would probably have the central unity and drama that it now lacks. There doubtless would be greater satirical meaning in the trivia of masterful scenes of a poker game or musicale or dialogues between pseudointellectuals and petty merchants. *Caetés* would then be a truly superior novel of the Northeast in both the documentary and artistic sense.

II São Bernardo

São Bernardo was published in 1934, one year after *Caetés*. The latter had been completed in 1928, however, which accounts for the remarkable progress found in *São Bernardo*. Again, the first person is used, but this time the narrator is conscious that he is telling his own story as a novel. In *Caetés* João Valério was attempting to write another book, until he realized that what he had observed and experienced made this project futile. The other book was of some value to João Valério as he planned it, and the symbolic parallel that it offered with the narrator's society remained artistically and philosophically useful to the reader. João Valério's observations and experiences turned out to be *Caetés*, whose utility was to show all of life in Palmeira dos Indios to be futile. After a short introduction that is part of *São Bernardo*, Paulo Honório begins to write his memoirs, and from the start the reader accompanies him in his efforts to recollect and compose his life in this form. In the first two chapters, which are a kind of prologue, the narrator and principal character of the novel confides to the reader; he is going to give

. . . an honest account of his life, however painful it may be. At first Paulo Honório had thought to distribute the various tasks to more learned collaborators, but they had too many literary prejudices; furthermore, one might add, the story was not theirs. Rude as he is, the master of São Bernardo is not unaware of other basic esthetic needs such as selection and reinforcement. Although he is evidently a person of some moral fiber, Paulo Honório's purpose in writing is not an obviously moral one; indeed, he does not know why he writes, but one senses his vital need to tell the story. He wants to tell a maximum of all the truth about himself with a minimum of false literature. Paulo Honório is a Brazilian Modernist at his humanistic best.[3]

Throughout, the narrator is virtually the sole center of interest and creator of all that is contained in *São Bernardo*. Although Machado de Assis had made very similar use of narrators in *Memórias Póstumas de Bras Cubas* (Posthumous Memoirs of Bras Cubas) and

Dom Casmurro, Graciliano's novel was considered unique in its day in this respect.

Paulo Honório's manner is brief, direct, and seemingly crude, as befits the strong, unlettered man that he purports to be. Everything and everyone pales before him. Yet he is possessed by as well as of a force. The acquisition and care of his property is Paulo Honório's passion, much in the tradition of Molière's Harpagon or Balzac's Grandet.

Once the prologue is over, the first-person narrative continues for the most part in a straight chronological line as Paulo Honório gives the reader his background. This prologue within the narrative presents the Naturalistic aspect, developed economically, impressionistically, with a good deal of cryptic humor, and withal quite completely. The protagonist's rise from obscure origins and his terse style are more reminiscent of the picaresque novel than of the "scientific" and emotional alternatives usually found in the works of other socio-political Brazilian Regionalists. Yet one is fully convinced throughout these eight chapters of Paulo Honório's social and psychological conditioning as he moves from *lazarillo* to master of São Bernardo by every opportunistic and criminal means accepted in his milieu. His success in acquiring and improving the *fazenda* on the Northeastern Littoral has resulted from a true struggle for survival, against rivals deserving of no pity, and from much hard work. He is not, however, the completely bestialized anti-hero of Naturalistic determinism, although this may be the more or less conscious opinion he has of himself even before his tragic experiences.[4]

Paulo Honório's tenderness for his *fazenda* and his dry sense of humor give some evidence of his humanity, however repressed. His desire to look after Margarida, the old Negress who raised him, although expressed in terms of repaying a material debt, is additional evidence. Otherwise, only São Bernardo draws the narrator's paternalistic attention, and it is with the wish to become a patriarch for its sake that he thinks of marrying.

Once in love, Paulo Honório begins to find a cure for his monomania, but his marital troubles have their roots in it, too; matters will get worse before they get better.

Chapter XIX is an important interruption in the transitional section of fourteen chapters dealing with Paulo Honório's fateful meeting with Madalena, their courtship, and early married life. It serves to remind the reader that this is merely the narration of past events and at the same time to point to the future within the narrative. Paulo Honório is emotionally disturbed as he attempts to remember, but his partial recollections and confusion with the present successfully whet the reader's curiosity and prepare him for tragedy. Further, the narrator's confession of guilt and ignorance with respect to his wife — and he emphasizes that the environment and Madalena must share the blame — as well as his declared need to unburden himself, predispose the reader to pity. Paulo Honório recognizes his wife's fine qualities, but his numerous prejudices make him find many defects in her. She is strong-willed and not the most communicative or tactful of wives, but her unpardonable fault to the reader is her neglect of the son she has borne Paulo Honório. Life has already become very difficult for them when, because of his great feelings of inferiority, the real seeds of tragedy are sown. One quite naturally thinks of Othello and Dom Casmurro in Chapters XXV - XXXI, which are an admirable study in the classical tradition of the terrible jealousy involuntarily nurtured by Paulo Honório's love and self-love.[5]

Despite his sincere recognition of Madalena's virtues, Paulo Honório does not understand his wife and necessarily presents her sketchily to the reader, somewhat as Dom Casmurro presents Capitu. Classically, she must have some flaw in order to deserve her fate. However, Madalena's defect in her husband's eyes is the modern assumption that she will share in the governance of São Bernardo. Not only does Paulo Honório find it impossible to break old habits, but he feels threatened by his wife's superior education. As she translates her humanitarian ideals into small acts of charity, he fears that she will ruin them. Paulo Honório's reactions are exteriorized and concentrated in a real-life rival for Madalena's affections, so that he may assert himself and dominate as he has always dominated. Whereas Dom Casmurro seems to enjoy a hollow victory, the master of São Bernardo does not. As we have seen, he loses the wife that he loved and, at the conclusion of the narrative, is in the process of losing most of his material wealth and power.

At the same time, however, Paulo Honório is gaining new strength, and he will have an heir, if not for São Bernardo, for his newfound humanity. Just as before the *fazenda* was the means and end of fulfillment, so now it is São Bernardo. The narrator, above all a strong personality who must create, creates uniquely. Originality is the mark of this personality, as of his creator. It seems unlikely that any of Graciliano's fellow citizens in Palmeira dos Indios could have produced *Caetés*, although the work is not very remarkable; it is more likely in the context of the novel that someone other than João Valério might have written *Caetés*. Paulo Honório conquers his environment as much as he is conquered by it. Aware of and reacting to his life at all times, he is stronger and more interesting than João Valério.

The reader always finds this Paulo Honório in the style of *São Bernardo*. In another chapter I have pointed out how the narrator's attitude toward the surroundings changes, and how they change accordingly. Although his language has certain constants that reflect this no-nonsense character, it follows an evolution that matches that of the man who is supposed to be using it. Paulo Honório always speaks or writes briefly, to the point, dynamically. His Portuguese is invariably correct, but tends to be fragmentary; and it is expressive, whether by its colloquialism or its crudity. He resembles Graciliano in vivid character delineation and masterful dialogue. As master of São Bernardo, Paulo Honório often speaks harshly and violently. When he gains practice in writing, the improvement coinciding with greater elevation of thought and spirit, his expression becomes fuller and approaches the lyrical.

Chapter XXXI contains the climactic scene of the tragedy, and is especially significant in that it marks the transition of Paulo Honório from *fazendeiro* to authentic human being. His record of the events shows him to be a great writer as well. The Romantic setting in the dead of a windy night, in a church where Madalena has been praying, is moving because of its sobriety. The dialogue is sparse and tense; during the long silences Paulo Honório wins a desperate struggle to restrain his passions. It is as though he already knows what he is soon to learn about Madalena's fidelity, her imminent suicide, and his tragic loss. After a period of apprenticeship with the works of important novelists and experimentation in basic techniques, Graciliano discovered the secret of creating language that not only is appropriate to but makes a character.

III   Angústia

Angústia shares some of the features of *Caetés* and *São Bernardo*. Some critics first thought that Graciliano was returning to the style of his first novel. Superficially there is some resemblance, but this is merely because both narrators are better educated than Paulo Honório and versed in traditional rhetoric. In fact, it has been noted that the narrator of *São Bernardo* makes abundant use of techniques found in *Caetés* to produce special effects. Indeed, Graciliano is again following the artistic principle of suiting the language of the character to his psychology and needs. Whereas this basic verisimilitude of all great classical and Realistic literature escaped some critics, all were and are impressed by Graciliano's innovative structures befitting and contributing to the more sensational themes of his new book. Despite personal preferences, most readers agree that *São Bernardo* and *Angústia* are very different, each exhibiting new facets of the author, facets that sometimes recur as he experiments from work to work.

For the third time Graciliano uses the first person. As in *São Bernardo*, the protagonist exclusively is the center of interest and creates his own story. Luís da Silva is not strong like Paulo Honório, however, nor is he weak in the manner of the apathetic, cynical João Valério. His background is such that even more than his predecessors he shares in the pessimistic world view generally exposed in Graciliano's works. Luís is further conditioned by mental illness. Repressed, he nurtures his frustrations until they are all released in one concentrated act of vengeance, instead of adopting action as a way of life or choosing not to act at all. His particularly negative viewpoint, focused on himself as well as others, makes life so bitter and oppressive, so totally unbearable, that the reader senses that release must occur in a violent form. Unrelieved by the irony or objectivity of Graciliano's first novels, *Angústia* is a complete study in frustration employing a maximum of dramatic tension. Luís' gloomily lyrical narrative draws on resources that in 1936 were most novel in Brazilian letters.

In *Angústia* Graciliano abandons numbering chapters consecutively with all that such numbering implies regarding time and space. The sections of Luís' account, set off by asterisks alone, depend entirely on his confused mental state. Whatever shifts of perspective there are have only the logic of irrationality. Everything here is part of a confession, told subjectively in an interior monologue with little interruption for description or dialogue. There is virtually no indication that *Angústia* is being written for a public, that Luís will ever share his story with anyone else. In his consciousness the action can range over all the places that he has known, spanning his whole life. The comings and goings in Luís' mind dimly reveal conflicts with conditions, with other people, and within himself; from these efforts eventually will emerge a clearer picture of Luís' case and solutions to his problems. In contemporary theater and the movies graphic effects produce and complement such flashbacks which, in addition to providing background, depict the mental probings of the subject. The reader of *Angústia* and more recent novels must be quick to seize a change in name or tense or some other subtle clue. Even if he were well, Luís would require fewer means to be oriented in what is familiar to him. As it is, he cannot step out of his consciousness for a more objective view of things either for himself or the reader.

For one who knows something of Graciliano's life from other works of his or from secondary sources, it is obvious that of the novels *Angústia* offers the closest parallels to his biography. Luís' memories of childhood on his grandfather's *fazenda* in the *sertão* are essentially Graciliano's of his stay in Pernambuco. If the author uses only his recollections of life on the *fazenda* it is the better to emphasize the harshness of conditions in the *sertão* and its effects on Luís. Graciliano's personal experience here is recorded in *Infância* and utilized fully again in *Vidas Sêcas*. Apart from general characteristics in backgrounds or in their persons shared by the author and his protagonist, from *Memórias do Cárcere* especially the reader learns of a number of particulars that lead him to take *Angústia* for a possible autobiography, or at least a work produced while Graciliano was in prison. In fact, it was the publication of this novel, written shortly before his incarceration, that preoccupied Graciliano intermittently during this time; he feared that the work was bad and longed to be able to revise it. Deprecation of his writing is as typical of Luís as of his creator. The narrator of *Angústia* suffers terribly over the pages that he grinds out to supplement his pay, while his best literature is at the mercy of rats in the wardrobe. Graciliano seems to have felt much the same way, more about some books than others; yet he needed a public also. Both Luís and Graciliano are fastidious in toilette, jealous of privacy, modest in sexual matters. Repressed and frustrated from childhood, each in his own context is obliged to live in filth and promiscuity. Mixed emotions that range from feelings of violation to inadequacy to prurience all bespeak a degree of morbidity in each. Seemingly incapacitated by pain and depression, they not only survive but succeed in curious ways.

Besides the frustrations already mentioned, to which Graciliano was able to give relief more satisfactorily than Luís, the novelist projects an intense dislike of bourgeois values in life and art through his creation. Whereas Luís is at last able to triumph violently over the man who embodies everything that he hates and envies, Graciliano vents his spleen in a more regular, healthier manner through writing as well as rebellions in a minor key outside of art. At both conscious and subconscious levels, Luis da Silva remains Graciliano Ramos' most complete projection of himself in an essentially fictional work.

IV   Vidas Sêcas

Vidas Sêcas is structurally very different from Graciliano's other novels. This difference, brought about accidentally, soon came to be required by the theme. Much to his surprise, one of a number of short pieces produced by Graciliano after his release from prison, the one that became the chapter on the dog, Baleia, was published in a Sunday supplement. Again to his surprise, it was received favorably, and he was led to assemble other pieces and write some new ones with a view to creating another novel. The work is thus composed of brief narratives linked together later by the author rather than conceived as a whole. Chapters may be detached and read as separate units, then, although they have the peculiar defect found in collections of Graciliano's short pieces. Apparently self-sufficient in the novel, they seem fragmentary when taken out of context. Like the "short stories," they lack the concentrated development of this genre and are incomplete out of a broader, unifying view. Indeed, singly or in groups, they represent different points of view that must converge to give the desired total perspective that is the author's.

Wishing to be more objective than in previous works, autobiographically speaking as well as with respect to his protagonists, Graciliano now abandons the first person for the third. He has two reasons for choosing greater objectivity, however, and therefore varies his utilization of the third person. One use is to have the reader acquire perception from the outside, of one character in diverse settings and different ones in the same environment, with variations. It is then the responsibility of the viewer of this series of clear, distinct tableaux to relate the segments, without too much involvement in inner drama. From this perspective the whole approaches the epic stature of Euclides da Cunha's *Os Sertões* (Rebellion in the Backlands), more compact in proportions but no less telling in its presentation of the *sertanejo* and his region.

Graciliano employs the third person also to lend *Vidas Sêcas* a tragic dimension in a more intimate manner than was possible in *Os Sertões*. The third person would not seem to permit the author to penetrate his characters as well as the first, but the indirect monologues created by Graciliano are most effective in this sense. Not only is the reader not immediately aware in these passages of the third rather than the first person, but may realize from how the protagonists address themselves and react to the surroundings that the third person is proper to them. Theirs is a primitive view of things, pure in its innocence and naïveté. They do not comprehend themselves except as part of the environment, determined by it, interacting with it, attempting to act upon it only in desperation, never really affecting it. Thus, they are as objective in their way as the author.

Graciliano has apparently not exercised here the great virtuosity needed for the highly dramatic first-person narratives of *São Bernardo* and especially *Angústia*. The structure of *Vidas Sêcas* is extremely simple, then, its style and tone appropriately unsophisticated. Formally, the design of the work coincides perfectly with the author's subject and theme. The book seems therefore as conditioned as Fabiano or Graciliano. With *Vidas Sêcas*, the author of *Caetés* indeed produced the superior, if most curious, novel of Northeastern Regionalism. It develops the determinism of *Os Sertões* in realistic prose without being merely a social document. It reveals all of the ills that continue to plague the *sertão* without becoming a political manifesto. Paradoxically, when it was clearest that Graciliano had mastered fictional narrative in its highest form, he turned his talents and new objectivity to the most personal kind of art, autobiography.

V   Insônia

Before discussing Graciliano's purely autobiographical works, however, I shall examine some of his "short stories." These are seldom mentioned in a consideration of Graciliano Ramos and, when they are, it is usually to dismiss them as of little value. In fact, he is normally thought of as a novelist only. The autobiographies, although acknowledged as great art, are generally treated as references, primary for Graciliano's life and times, secondary for his novels which, ironically, are autobiographical to a large extent. As I have already indicated, it is unfair to deal with *Infância* and the *Memórias* in this manner exclusively, but it seems unwise to overlook the short narratives at least as important sources. Artistically, there is a close relationship between them and *Vidas Sêcas* and *Infância* in particular; and biographically speaking, the association is closest between the stories and the two autobiographies.

That the pieces under examination here, collected in *Insônia* (1947), are unsuccessful as short stories is suggested by the title under which Graciliano first published most of them in volume form:

Histórias Incompletas (1946). Many of them, written during their author's incarceration or shortly after his release and appearing in periodicals either in Brazil or Argentina, indeed seem incomplete. They often resemble the Brazilian *crônica* which most commonly is the author's personal commentary on some aspect of reality, routine or extraordinary, much as in the American "column." More than slices of life, they nevertheless approach the Naturalistic technique of capturing scenes, types, activities observed and recorded by the writer, but fragmentary out of a broader context. Pieces like Baleia's narrative take on fuller meaning when inserted in a longer work such as *Vidas Sêcas*. Yet the latter is little more than a collection of such narratives more or less related by Graciliano and his reader.

The pieces in *Insônia* have like similarities of technique, but also of subject, theme, and tone. Whether conveyed in a direct or indirect, exterior or interior monologue, each tends to be the perspective of an unfortunate being on what oppresses him. Whatever the appearances, the characters are always victims of circumstances over which they have no control. The atmosphere is usually one of nightmarish unreality, caused by insomnia, delirium, or some strong emotion. In such an atmosphere conventional notions of space and time break down. The disturbed mind makes free, random movements, it seems, but frequent references to the chiming of clocks and other stimuli from the outside serve to demonstrate the existence of that other world. Determined by it, the tormented, unhealthy individual seeks to escape from it and minimize its ill effects, customarily without success. I shall analyze some samples of the deformations that preoccupy Graciliano.

"Insônia," which lends its name to and sets the mood of the collection, is followed by "Um Ladrão" (A Thief). This narrative seems to have been inspired by anecdotes told to Graciliano by a colorful thief whom he met in prison. In the *Memórias do Cárcere* Gaúcho explains and illustrates his *modus operandi* directly to Graciliano, who reports it. "Um Ladrão" has this material worked into the narrative written as the indirect monologue of a novice thief whose mentor is Gaúcho. From the impression that he is able to piece together, the reader can easily imagine the author, had he continued to steal coins from his father in order to buy books, in the role of the young man. In general, he resembles Graciliano's protagonists physically and emotionally, exhibiting similar nervous habits, psychosomatic manifestations, perception of the surroundings, and reactions toward others and himself.

Apprehensive as he is before and during the crime, it is expected that the thief's consciousness be exaggeratedly keen. Yet he has the air of a somnambulist about him from the beginning. Involuntarily he recalls scenes from the past that haunt him, scenes already familiar to Graciliano's reader from other works. Because of inexperience the thief controls himself and the situation badly, and the reader is not surprised to have him berate himself as he fears Gaúcho would if he could see him. Both the protagonist and reader know, of course, that Gaúcho too has made mistakes and been imprisoned a number of times. In order to avoid ridicule, however, the young man plans to escape to a suburb where he can open a quiet café with the money that he is stealing. The reader anticipates that the thief will suffer a denouement like that of La Fontaine's milkmaid.

Indeed, after his gaucheness and a fit of nervous coughing, the young man experiences a certain euphoria at his good luck; but at the same time he indulges in more self-criticism. Instead of leaving the scene of his crime, he retraces his steps in order to prove that he can do a better job without the aid of chance. Suddenly, repressed sexual desire — suggested by the recurring vision from his past of the girl with braids and green eyes — comes to the fore. Unable to restrain himself, the thief returns to the bedroom where the girl with the exposed bosom sleeps and he kisses her on the mouth. The alarm is sounded, he awakens from his trance and runs, only to fall down the stairs. During his fall he has another kind of nightmare, this time of what will happen to him after he is arrested and of prison life. When he awakens from this vision, it has faded but is replaced by the beginnings of the real-life experience known to the reader of the *Memórias*.

Narrated in the first person and capturing Graciliano's memories of his illness in 1932, "O Relógio do Hospital" (The Hospital Clock) is one of several related pieces. "Paulo" (Paul) is almost a repetition of this narrative; "Insônia," told also in the first person, deals with a condition very like an illness; and a clock, among other devices, plays a role in the third-person "Um Ladrão" as important as in the other three selections. "O Relógio do Hospital" is more unified than the other two first-person accounts around the central figure of the narrator, although it does not have a story line to the same degree as "Um Ladrão." Like much of Graciliano's work, this piece records the comings and goings of a consciousness, now viewing the individual's surroundings, now considering what preoccupies it in different time zones. The consciousness is more or less objective and follows this or that pattern, depending on the physical and mental state of the subject and what is affecting him most during the narration.

As the selection opens the narrator is about to undergo a serious operation. Both because of his physical condition and the treatment normally given to a hospital patient, he feels very detached. Before and after the operation he is concerned about what is happening to him, but is so helpless that he cannot participate except in a way that seems objective. Yet there is something unreal about his extreme passivity. The narrator wishes to see his slippers by the bed in order to reestablish contact with reality, if such exists in concrete form.

Repeatedly, other elements contribute to the patient's sense of unreality, variously as he is in pain, delirious, or sedated. Again, the disagreeable present revives unpleasant memories: scenes of school, members of the family, an interview with a politician, a visit to a prostitute. Always the narrator experiences insecurity and inadequacy, and this is a fact of life for Graciliano and his protagonists. Sounds and other stimuli reaching the patient are distorted, sometimes representing different sounds, sometimes undergoing stranger metamorphoses. He hears the slow, rickety clock as his grandfather's nagging voice when he taught him spelling. The silence of the clock is significant, too, for he interprets it as the death of a fellow patient, and perhaps his own. The frightful vision of a leper's face haunts the narrator. He first imagines the wretch's laments, which soon become the snakes that troubled him as a child; later they are transformed into the equally imaginary laments of a child in the charity ward. Thoughts of the morgue and dissection recur in the patient's mind, for them and for himself. Street noises create images of the people there, their problems, and those that may be his when he is out in the world again. Like Graciliano, the narrator concerns himself with his own suffering and that of all humanity with which it is confused. The only solution for the patient seems to be "dilution," or fusion, with his environment as he loses consciousness and the sounds of the hospital, including the awful ticking of the clock, fade away.

After the interior dialogues of "O Relógio do Hospital" and "Paulo," the reader finds the third person again in "Luciana" and "Minsk." A pair of narratives related much as the chapters of *Vidas Sêcas* are related, they have the same characters with somewhat different focus and manner from one to the other. "Luciana" offers a slice from the life of a small girl who successfully avoids parental repression by repeated flights into the outer world as well as by playacting. Graciliano combines indirect monologue to present the inner world of the child and the objective third person for more exterior aspects of her life. The piece is fragmentary, however, and the reader would appreciate fuller development to learn if Luciana continues her little triumphs or grows to be more like Graciliano as a child. "Minsk," on the other hand, is rather closer to the convention of the short story. Luciana and other characters from the first selection are still important, but attention is on the parrot Minsk as much as on the girl herself. Except that an animal is one of the central figures, there is slight resemblance to "Baleia" until the few touches of the very end. Hence Graciliano's stance as the omniscient author throughout most of the narrative.

The story begins when Uncle Severino brings Minsk as a present for Luciana. A description of the parrot's feathers "adorning a tremulous life" is a nice figure that seems to contain as much prophecy as poetry. The intimacy springing up between the girl and Minsk and the activities of the bird occupy most of the middle part of the story. A brief section explaining Luciana's curious, stubborn habit of walking backwards with eyes closed prepares the reader for the tragic end. She steps on and mortally wounds the one she has come to love most. In his last few moments of life, as Luciana comes to grips with what she has done, Minsk appears to suffer at the separation and to want to console her. Thus, he seems to share the feelings and sense of responsibility experienced by Baleia at the time of her death.

"Dois Dedos" (Two Fingers) is again an indirect monologue and takes its name from the reasons that Dr. Silveira gives his wife for his visit to the governor. He and the important man were school chums, as close as the nail to the flesh in which it is imbedded, as equal as the middle can be made to the index finger. These are paraphrases of expressions and gestures repeated by the protagonist during the narrative. Along with other repetitions, they underscore the thoughts that recur in the doctor's mind, the changes that have taken place over twenty years, especially the transformation during the visit, and the final dramatic irony.

Silveira's wife warns her husband that he and the governor have nothing in common, that he had best stay home. The doctor insists that his old friend would be offended if he did not pay his respects, brushes his worn clothes, and sets off in a rented car. No sooner does he arrive than he realizes that his wife was right, amid growing feelings of inferiority and inadequacy as he copes with grim functionaries, suspicious guards, highly polished floors, oversized furniture, and finally the governor himself in his huge office. In vain does Silveira relive a past in which he was superior to his old friend, who failed in chemistry, and intimate with his family. They have grown apart physically, not seeing each other, each belonging to a different socioeconomic class; time has made them unrecognizable, to themselves and to one another, as the young men they were twenty years ago.

Magnificence, enormity, indifference overwhelm the modest doctor. Repeatedly he fears slipping on the varnished floor. Entirely out of place, he worries about his behavior. Frequent reference is made to the governor's puffy, impatient eyes and their failure to recognize his former schoolmate. Disoriented, intimidated, the near-comic Silveira no longer knows himself and acts as the bureaucracy expects people to act when they visit the governor. The doctor had no intention of asking favors when he left home. Gradually conditioned by the insidious new atmosphere, as though hypnotized by the governor's unattractive eyes, he protests to himself that he is not there for the usual reason. Finally, ironically, sadly, the doctor involuntarily concludes his visit by requesting the governor to find him a post in Public Health. Typically, Graciliano seems to suggest that the "two fingers," despite their transformations, are still "two fingers," although perhaps the middle and index have changed places.

In "Silveira Pereira" Graciliano again uses the first person, in a direct monologue that may well have been inspired by his own student days in Maceió. Typically, the narrator has no name. His personality is clearly that of a young man trying to find himself and to impress others with his maturity. The absence of interior dialogue prevents him from being as striking as some of Graciliano's characters; but he does not have problems as serious as theirs. He is quite honest with himself and his reader, as in a diary. Youth tends to make one ingenuous, but the extreme ingenuousness of the narrator here may owe something to the author's ironical treatment. Such objectivity reinforces the reader's suspicion that Graciliano recalls himself in his young protagonist.

The student has recently left home for school in the big city and lives in a boardinghouse with other typical residents. Most of these treat him with kind condescension when he puts on airs of sophistication, but he does not mind as long as they are kind. Only one boarder, the one in room nine, Pereira or Silveira or Silveira Pereira, will not help him to become a man, an intellectual, a *littérateur*. When he thinks number nine a man of letters, the narrator abandons his studies to write a short story; but the fat, colorless, heartless drudge reads it without comment. Feeling misunderstood, the student founds a newspaper to give himself importance and to print his work. Whatever or however he tries, he cannot put the man out of his mind. Even if he fails in school, he will write more stories, he will attract the attention and know the opinion of Pereira Silveira or Silveira Pereira. The boy must prove himself through the man who symbolizes the incomprehension and indifference of the adult world.

VI   Infância

No doubt there is some overlap of time during which the narratives of *Insônia* (1947) and the episodes of *Infância* (1945) were written. The same is true of *Vidas Sêcas* (1938) and *Memórias do Cárcere* (1953). By his own admission Graciliano was preoccupied with the publication of *Angústia* and the composition of several narratives while in prison, and he took notes for the *Memórias,* although he destroyed these before writing the memoirs. Similarities in content and form from one of Graciliano's works to the next have been noted more than once, as well as the growing tendency to deal in frankly autobiographical terms, in relatively short pieces much like the *Essais* of Montaigne. Whether in the first or third person, whether inserted in a longer narrative or left separate, all are to be interpreted as based on the author's own life or observations that together give his view of Northeastern Brazil. The use of the first person throughout *Infância* gives the book a kind of unity that *Insônia* does not have; but the direct monologue lacks the depth of the interior monologue and sometimes even of the indirect monologue in the third person found in that collection and elsewhere. The perspective is intended to be that of a child, one who often suffers, but one who does not yet have the serious problems that may plague him as a Luís da Silva. Like Fabiano's, the childlike mind perceives the world as a series of tableaux with episodic action loosely centered about its person. Only when the child acquires greater sophistication, and if his mind remains healthy, will he have the wisdom to achieve an integrated perspective. Not to be overlooked in the process of integration is the role of the author, sometimes discreet, sometimes disarmingly obvious, nor that of the reader.

The first selection, entitled "Nuvens" (Clouds), is representative of how the author collects his material somewhat hazily, as through a screen of clouds that sometimes opens, sometimes not. A jar filled with the fruit of a *pitombeira* is the first thing that he seems to recall, imperfectly, and he might think it a dream if it did not lead to other associations; or did he tell others about it and they help him keep it vivid? At any rate, *pitomba* came to mean any spherical object for him, and he was disturbed when the error of his generalization was explained. Like anyone who tries to go back in memory to his earliest childhood, Graciliano finds a jumble of faces and words. That he remembers anything is not to be attributed to extraordinary intelligence. Deprecating himself in this, as it is customary for him to do in most respects, the author nevertheless recalls some things very clearly. He especially fixes scenes in a school where he and his family spent some time while on the trip from Alagoas to Pernambuco. Although he knows them all to be of the same time and place, some faces and objects stand out, others do not, all of which he explains to the reader who goes back with him in time. The whole is presented in random fashion, impressionistically, emphasizing the senses and emotions by which memories have been kept alive. Thus Graciliano assembles portraits of his parents. Their hands are important among the images that stay with him, but also the sounds that help him recall those hands that inspired obedience and respect. Other sounds of *sertanejo* violence and the fear instilled by them are equally a part of the author's recollections of childhood. Yet life in the harsh *sertão* was not without its rewards in nature and society. Graciliano continues to recall those hands and the sounds accompanying them in gentler moments. There were also the unsophisticated games, stories, and songs of his parents and their rough folk. Tongue in cheek, the author chides himself for liking the rebellious young hero of a popular satirical piece only when transformed by literature. There is much that can be confronted only at a distance through the objectivity presumably conferred by time and art.

Many interesting chapters follow that gradually complete Graciliano's picture of life in the *sertão,* its rhythm that is so dependent on the climate, the types that compose its society and his family, and their problems. Above all there are those elements that most affected the author as an individual when he was a child. After the first chapter Graciliano largely abandons the device of explaining the process whereby he backtracks, merely offering the reader his recollections as clear and distinct. Yet the loose construction and grouping of short chapters, with numerous digressions to describe whatever has been suggested, remind the alert reader of Graciliano's impressionistic process and its goals.

As Graciliano probes his memory, recaptures images, meditates on and reshapes them, he acquires greater understanding of his past. Given the nature of this past and the author's, the picture that he paints is essentially a somber one. Yet his increased understanding includes sympathy also, for others as well as himself. I have already pointed out the probable affinity that existed between Graciliano and a grandfather. The well-known unflattering portraits of his parents are softened by an explanation of how they were able to subdue their difficult temperaments with each other sufficiently to be compatible. The reader inevitably thinks of Fabiano when he sees the tragic effects of the *sêca* on the head of Graciliano's family; a shopkeeper himself, the memorialist must have felt even more keenly the trials that his father experienced in this occupation. Portraits are further tempered by touches of comedy, sometimes satirical or ironical, but sometimes just for fun. Graciliano points a finger of ridicule at some of his mother's religious notions and literary tastes, but also at his own when he was a child. As for the time he got tipsy and made a fool of himself with the ladies during a visit with his parents to a neighboring *fazenda,* the anecdote, for all the serious elements that are interspersed, is an amusing one.

Yet the character sketches and episodes evoked by Graciliano's memory are fashioned by his art into a panorama of life that tends to confirm the general pessimism of all his work. Victims and oppressors alike seldom triumph over conditions or themselves. Among the victims there are those few who are wholly good and do good, despite their lot. The oppressors include those who are wholly bad. More likely, of course, is a mixture of good and evil as in real life. In Graciliano's world individuals are still more likely to have more evil than good in them. If they are not completely brutalized, however, they have some feeling for right and wrong, and in this moral sense there may be hope for suffering humanity.

In the famous episode where Graciliano first has a taste of his father's belt, the author prepares the background by explaining other beatings that he received; how, although he was always made to feel guilty, they seemed natural simply because might makes right; and that once the pain left him the beating was more or less forgotten. He is extremely generous in forgiving his mother who, irritated but without malice, once beat him badly with a knotted rope, thereby incurring her mother's censure. Moreover, his mother was sorry for what she had done, the blame was less hers than the knots', and the incident would be closed were it not for the other case. What makes the latter memorable in its own right, and so much more horrifying, seems to be an utter disregard for justice added to the customary irrational violence. Awakening in a bad humor and unable to find the belt that he misplaced, Graciliano's father mumbles a question to him. The father's rage mounts as he repeats the question over and over, distinctly now, and the child's panic grows so that he could not answer even if he knew how. Finding the belt, his father is not content, but uses it to beat Graciliano. The author notes signs indicating then as now that the father is later ashamed of his behavior. That he cannot bring himself to apologize or express regret makes the fault triply unforgivable. Graciliano doubtless expects more of his father than of his mother, and this is another reason for recalling the event as his first experience with "justice." Nonetheless, he records the fact that his father was not totally without conscience.

The same saving grace cannot always be found in the gallery of sadistic bullies of all walks of life who punish often masochistic children or childlike creatures in *Infância*. Graciliano accuses himself also of contributing to the misery of his fellows, partly to show how such perversion is in the natural order of things as he has come to know it, partly to highlight the social propaganda of this work. When his father beats his black companion and he feels compelled to participate even slightly, Graciliano states that were he successful in following his evil instinct he would perhaps become a "strong man." The father discovers that he is interfering, however, and turns his "justice" against the son. Rather, concludes Graciliano ironically, he is obliged to participate in another's suffering (as one always does whether deservedly or not?). On another occasion, when the poor tramp Venta Romba is to be imprisoned because of his parents' prejudice and position (the father is now a judge!), Graciliano is too cowardly to protest the injustice. He blames the incident for his later insolence at home, after he became exempt from punishment, and for his general lack of confidence in authority.

Graciliano is equally guilty of cowardice on several other occasions, however, especially involving classmates more brutalized than he. At one school it was Adelaide, a cousin from a wealthy branch of the family, born to be mistress of a plantation. On the one hand, her martyrdom at the hands of the mulatto schoolteacher and the latter's family is described from the viewpoint of Graciliano the boy, who hated the teacher and was not overly fond of blacks. On the other, Graciliano the man and sometime propagandist explains the reversal of roles as class struggle and revenge. At another school it was a boy to whom the author refers only as "An Unhappy Child," abused cruelly by everyone at home and at school. Graciliano's pathos and moral purpose here are worthy of a Dickens or a Zola. In fact, the moral clearly implied in the conclusion matches the anonymity of the subject well and makes a kind of morality of the chapter. An unhappy child can easily become an enemy of society and come to an untimely end. In view of his own unhappy childhood, it must be considered fortunate that Graciliano was not an enemy of society in the same sense. That what he was by nature and conditioning made him in some sense an enemy of society is true, however, as is the fact that society retaliated by imprisoning him and contributing to his early death.

It must be assumed that Graciliano was an exceptional child in several respects. How normal or abnormal were his reactions to rude *sertanejo* life? How much does the adult Graciliano color his recollections of that culture for artistic, philosophical, or even propagandistic effects? Although the objectivity of *Infância* may be questioned on these several grounds, Graciliano undoubtedly had a number of harrowing experiences as a child. One of the first to try him is a repulsive eye infection that causes him to feel rejection by family and friends. In his periodic blindness and discomfort, emotional as well as physical, he naturally becomes introverted, given to morbidity and excesses of imagination.

On another occasion his black companion João takes him to view the ruins of a fire in which a young black woman died saving the last of the family possessions, an image of the Virgin Mary. The mere thought of such a destructive fire first arouses the boy's curiosity, but when he witnesses its ravages on the corpse he is repelled. So hideous is the sight that he talks about it repeatedly, in great detail, as he now writes about it. For all his parents' pious consolations, the boy wonders how the Virgin could allow such a thing to happen to a devoted servant. The adult perhaps more than the boy wonders why it was preferable for the poor cabin to be destroyed than the church or a shop in town; and how the black girl, despite her Purgatory on earth, could be allowed into Heaven in what is now a repugnant state after all. More important here than any antireligious criticism is the social commentary.

Equally shattering, and described in terms that seem as morbid, are the young Graciliano's attendance at a child's funeral, his coming upon an ossuary, and the emotional aftermath. His faith is shaken, not in God of Whom he has no thought, but in souls; yet his soul does not die completely, as he puts it, and he continues to be visited by phantoms. It is difficult to speak with certainty of the religious beliefs, if any, of the boy or man Graciliano, but he was skeptical of much in this as well as in other areas. Surprisingly absent from Graciliano's work is the anticlerical feeling so typical of Brazilian males. In fact, he seems to have had a rather high opinion of the priests that he knew. Their simplicity, honesty, and even heroism, qualities that discouraged vocations among the gentry accustomed to moral laxity in clerics, attracted Graciliano. According to one chapter of *Infância,* he even thinks of entering the seminary at one point. Graciliano questions the literal truth of the Scriptures taught him by Father Pimentel, however, as any reasonable person may, and is easily distracted.

Finally, another episode must be mentioned to which Graciliano appears to react supersensitively. Despite some passing initiation to sex on the *fazendas* where the boy spent a considerable part of his childhood, he seems not to know the facts of life very well. Referring to his mother's pregnancies always in terms of her gaining weight and being ill, he appears surprised whenever she turns up a new baby. At the age of eleven, however, Graciliano is involved with a newspaper, a literary society, novels of dubious morality, Laura, and puberty. It seems to be a great deal with which to cope, particularly the suggestive literature, the girl, and his growing desire. Struggling with all of the normally mixed emotions of adolescence, the boy is ashamed of violating Laura's purity and his own in dreams that for him are nightmares. Like Luís da Silva or the adult Graciliano, he is obsessed with washing away the stains, real or imagined. At last a friend takes him to visit a prostitute, who inevitably infects him and, a bit sadly, all fantasies are dispelled. The adult Graciliano apparently felt ambivalent about women and sex. Desire revisited him periodically, and he satisfied it, fathering with his two wives numerous children of whom he was fond; yet there is often more than a hint of prudery in his references to sex. The eleven-year-old's painful visit to the whore recurs in modified form several times in his writings.

Among the several threads of subjects and themes that I have traced in *Infância,* there remains one that must be the most important for the reader to keep sight of. In spite of many obstacles, and partly because of some of these, Graciliano became a great creative force as a writer and a thinker. Concerning his art there can be no doubt. With regard to the negative philosophy that is usually most apparent, I have attempted to emphasize evidence and inter-

pretations that render it constructive in the long run. Witness
Graciliano's dreadful initiation to reading and literature. His father
first proposes schooling to the boy as an asset in business, begins to
teach him in the old-fashioned punitive way against his wishes, then
turns him over to equally harsh disciplinarians in the local schools.
Graciliano will be plagued also with the hypocrisy and
irrelevance of school texts, ranging from unrealistic moral pieces
for primers to the great classics such as Camões. With some help
from his mother, oddly enough, other more kindly disposed relatives,
and one unusually humane schoolmistress, he overcomes fear,
frustration, and boredom. Progress in reading leads to progress in
other areas. Submitting that the teacher will not be fairly treated
because she is an "anarchist," Graciliano is saying that her relatively
laissez-faire attitude with pupils will not be appreciated by the
authorities. Dona Maria has liberated reading and the wisdom that
this can bring. Another time, the boy experiences difficulty in
pronouncing "Samuel Smiles," the name of an author encountered
in a class text. Both he and the teacher of the moment, one of many
incompetents to whom Graciliano is exposed, bluff the pronuncia-
tion whenever the name turns up. He finally learns the correct
English sounds from a tutor with whom he now has private lessons.
Later, in his father's shop, the name comes to be mispronounced by
the superior types who frequent the place and torment Graciliano.
They sneer when he corrects them, of course, but his own knowledge
of superiority is enough triumph for him. Henceforth he can take
refuge in his books without cowardice; he is very grateful to Samuel
Smiles, dull reading though he may be.

The boy becomes interested in Romantic novels in roundabout
fashion also. One evening his father orders him to read aloud. The
literary style is unfamiliar and difficult, relations with his father are
strained, and the reading goes badly. Instead of flying into a rage,
however, the father begins to explain the material. These sessions
continue for several evenings, and painful as they are, the boy looks
forward to them. He is dismayed when his father loses interest, for
he wants to finish the novel. When Graciliano turns to his cousin
Emília, she urges him to be courageous and independent. If
astronomers can read the heavens, he can unravel the mysteries of
his book; and he takes her advice. Another time, Emília causes
Graciliano unexpected frustration. He is reading a novel about a
lonely boy and his dog. Unfortunately, the book is by a Protestant,
and according to Emília Graciliano's soul is in grave danger. At first

rebellious that his newfound freedom through reading should be cur-
tailed, he is finally crushed by the enormity of circumstances. Not
only must the lonely boy Graciliano be confined in every way as in a
cage, but he cannot be consoled by reading about that other lonely
boy. Graciliano was to find companionship in the protagonists of his
own works to compensate for the confinement and loneliness of the
boy and man.

It should be noted that, whereas once being taught to read was a
punishment in every way, now impediments to reading and the
liberation that it brings make Graciliano weep. "Laura," the final
chapter of *Infância,* is one that records Graciliano's approaching
maturity most fully, in more ways than one, as I suggested earlier.
Like most of the chapters in this and other works, it steeps the reader
in Graciliano's pessimism. Throughout life individuals struggle in
varying degrees and with varying success against the conditions that
determine them. Their efforts are mostly vain, either making them
ridiculous or bringing greater evil. At times they have the illusion of
lessening the weight of the chain of negative links woven by blind
fate; but this simply means that the weight has been temporarily
shifted, perhaps to someone else, only to fall back all the more
heavily on its original bearer. Illusory or not, the efforts will and
should continue, for the only positive meaning recognized by
Graciliano in a basically corrupt, unhappy system comes in the form
of good works. His awareness of the state of affairs, attempts at
enlightenment, and need to share burdens for the sake of others and
his own were his refuge. Graciliano's life was devoted to propagating
his philosophy through art. *Infância* gives evidence that, fortunately,
there were such as the local postmaster and notary, among others,
perhaps few in number but very significant, who helped him along
the way to become a "strong man" through good instincts and
literature.

VII   Memórias do Cárcere

Graciliano's *Memórias do Cárcere* are, like *Infância,* a useful ad-
junct to a clearer understanding of his first works. The reader may
verify from them many of the author's personal characteristics and
experiences transposed into the protagonists of his novels. Considerably more important than *Infância* in revealing Graciliano
directly as a person, however, the *Memórias* are a better tool also for
grasping the writer. As he reshapes the material from which he could
least detach himself as a human being, Graciliano not only clarifies

the autobiographical elements in *Angústia,* but gives even as fictional a work as *São Bernardo* a much more personal aspect.

An author's most distinctive marks are, of course, found in his use of and views on language. It is known that Graciliano was always scrupulous with respect to grammatical correctness, precise terminology, and maximum economy, clarity, and honesty with decency. From the beginning of his career he worked steadily to restore color and significance to traditional rhetoric, and prestige to literary language after the abuses of the Modernists. I have already pointed out how, although Graciliano is not identical with his fictional protagonists, there is a close correlation between many of his points of view and theirs. All of them detest good speakers, partly because the latter's oratory is often so empty, partly because they themselves are frequently inarticulate.[6] Graciliano expresses himself directly on this score in numerous places in the *Memórias,* as for example when he compares the serious speeches of Rodolfo with the disorganized outpourings of Miranda. Similarly, João Valério criticizes Evaristo Barroca's pedantry, Paulo Honório Azevedo Gondim's artificial prose, and Luís da Silva Julião Tavares' pompous pronouncements.

Having been subject to much illness and therefore to many doctors, Graciliano often criticizes the unintelligible jargon that they tend to use with patients. On one occasion in the *Memórias* Graciliano thinks of consulting Dr. Hora, a fellow prisoner in the ship's hold where the author has just suffered a hemorrhage, but decides against it. Not reticent about the episode at the time of the writing, he is when ill, through lack of confidence in the doctor, who will be unable to help but who will use complicated terms in an attempt to spare him. These opinions, among others, are shared by Graciliano with João Valério. They seem to favor less formalism and greater authenticity in language as well as in the culture that it represents. Yet the author may well feel some ambivalence on the subject of culture. João Valério appears to take some pleasure in noting that, during the week that it takes Adrião to die, those keeping watch in his house have reverted to the stage of the savage Caetés because of fatigue and bad temper. Doubtless aware that in his first novel he has prophesied scenes such as the stinking hold of the *Manaus,* Graciliano asks whether that cross section of society in prison can remain civilized in pajamas, slippers, and using matches for toothpicks. He is perhaps less cynical but no less pessimistic when he observes that they have dropped many social habits formerly considered indispensable and are regressing involuntarily to a primitive state. No doubt the author realized much of the falseness in society and would like to see some facades torn down. At the same time he is a conservative, fastidious person, recognizing his many defenses but jealous of them.

Graciliano's inhibitions and regrets concerning his writing are analogous. Repeatedly he admits extreme difficulty in finding an idea, then clarifying and giving it form; a perfectionist, too, he is forever dissatisfied. Drinking coffee and smoking as he wrestles with the slow, arduous, and apparently unrewarding task of writing his memoirs in novel form, Paulo Honório resembles Graciliano (who like other protagonists adds alcohol to his stimulants). Luís da Silva makes scarcely any reference to the memoirs that he narrates, but criticizes the hack writing that he must do to live. Most like João Valério in art as well as philosophy, the author cannot write at all unless he has some direct experience with his subject. Not only does he insist that he cannot treat a purely imaginative subject with any plausibility, but *Infância* and the *Memórias* demonstrate to what extent the author's fiction is based on his own reality. So much is this the case that his public — reading that João Valério abandons his novel on the Caetés because the only one that he could write if he had the interest would deal with people of his acquaintance — believed that this was in fact what Graciliano had done in his unflattering picture of Palmeira dos Indios.[7] Although he lacks a certain kind of imagination, Graciliano confesses also that he is too analytical to be a complete Realist. Again like João Valério or Paulo Honório, his attention tends to fix itself on a few salient traits, physical or psychological. Hence portraits, except for that of the one main character, are impressionistic and modern. Concentration with the depth that results lends a classical quality as well to Graciliano's manner. The method of drawing portraits is reinforced by the intensity and abstraction produced as Graciliano, Paulo Honório, and especially Luís da Silva telescope circumstances in different time zones on which they fix their attention also. Despite his hesitation at the beginning of the *Memórias* to speak of real persons, then, Graciliano gives ample testimony elsewhere in the work of an incapacity to observe and record the whole person. Such "incapacity" ensures discretion and prevents art from becoming documentation.

From the purely human point of view, Graciliano seems closest to Fabiano of all his fictional protagonists. Fabiano's usual lack of sophistication and apparent inability to articulate, however, make him Graciliano's spokesman in a literary sense as well. The resemblance is particularly noticeable when Fabiano's reactions and mental processes occasionally become superior to what one comes to expect of him. I have pointed out how, in addition to the content of some chapters, the perspective and organization of *Infância* remind the reader especially of *Vidas Sêcas*. The themes and structures of the *Memórias* reveal further the closeness of Graciliano to Fabiano in many episodes that tell of the incredible humiliation endured by the author and his fellows in prison. The pain of this experience echoes that of Graciliano's childhood, recorded with his conclusions in *Infância* and prolonged throughout his life and other works. Graciliano and his protagonists isolate and insulate themselves against others, yet they do not like being "strangers" and must break into the outer world in one way or another.

Despite great culture, which he manifests often enough,[8] Graciliano's *sertanejo* characteristics again identify him most closely with Fabiano. He is by nature and conditioning somewhat rough, and it suits him to be so both in life and art. Believing life generally empty of real poetry, Graciliano mistrusts poetic literature and claims to be ignorant of it. It is known that he wrote and published verse, however, and he gives evidence of being a fine judge of poetry. Having experienced little of the gentler emotions, he feared superficial sentimentality. For all their repression and restraint, Graciliano and his protagonists can be tender as well as explosively passionate. Paulo Honório cares for his old foster mother and his son. Fabiano loves his family, however crudely, and Graciliano's style in *Vidas Sêcas,* e.g., his discreet use of diminutives, reveals affection for Fabiano's sons. In the *Memórias* Graciliano repeatedly shows a certain fondness and concern for his own wife and children; if he is grouchy or apathetic on occasion, circumstances as much as temperament are responsible.

The rude terms employed by the "cultivated backlander" are well known through his narrators in works of fiction and autobiography alike. Like other forms of disparagement, they are directed against the self as much as against others. More than masochistic or misanthropic, Graciliano's sufferings made him wish to be honest with everyone. If others are "burros," so is he at times, and he can send his own work to the devil as well as another's. Indeed, he is his own severest critic so that he can be severe with others. The situation at the conclusion of *Vidas Sêcas* seems to be repeated when Graciliano tells the reader that he will never return to Alagoas. He now realizes that his troubles have been the fault of a naïve presumption in thinking his efforts of any consequence. Fabiano's hope of a better life elsewhere, however, is absent in his creator, whose bitter irony in *Vidas Sêcas* is made evident from the *Memórias*. Finding no persons guilty, Graciliano nonetheless cannot absolve the dirty business in which all have become enmeshed. His proposed educational reforms would render too many incompetents unhappy. It is better that they continue to teach patriotic songs and otherwise make dolts of the children. Like Fabiano and others who suffer in Graciliano's books, the memorialist blames the system rather than the individuals who are its instruments. Nevertheless, his reactions must inevitably be directed against concrete persons. Resolutely negative concerning society, normally reserved with individuals even when he admires them, Graciliano seems most enthusiastic about humanity. In any case, the future Communist continues to care, which is to hope, and therefore to write, much as Fabiano sets out to seek a better life.

In the *Memórias,* then, as in all of Graciliano Ramos' career, there are two fundamental, contradictory tendencies. Graciliano the man, the several protagonists through whom he projects himself, and sometimes secondary characters too, are subject to many chaotic impulses. These are usually triggered from outside the individual. Sometimes actively, sometimes passively, he exercises his will against them. Paulo Honório's negativism is seen in his ruthless climb to wealth and power. Luís da Silva is antisocial in a passive way until he murders Julião Tavares and enters his delirium. Graciliano reacts much like the narrator of *Angústia,* rejecting his environment psychosomatically to the point of terminating many vital bodily functions. Graciliano the thinker and artist strives to dominate the confusion through clarity and harmony, and he imposes these controls on his creatures. The struggle between the two opposing currents is the basic theme of Graciliano's work and determines its structures. A simple, terse, clear style is the chief instrument employed by Graciliano to bring order out of chaos. If he does not succeed in every instance, it is because Graciliano's re-creation, like life, does not always succeed. If his characters do not triumph, or triumph only in a limited or ambiguous sense, it is because Graciliano's work must reflect life. Their efforts to succeed, largely through the medium placed at their disposal by the author, reflect life also. The struggle through a prolonged, highly tense period leads, however, from one extreme to its antithesis, as in classical drama.

In the *Memórias* the reader witnesses the struggle as it occurs in life and in art simultaneously. Graciliano's fictional works are transpositions of his personal observations, to be sure, but the *Memórias* attempt to present these in the most direct manner possible. Here reality, exterior or interior, is not composite in the usual artistic sense. Each part, whether recollections of Graciliano's own experience or that of others, is treated with utmost objectivity: conditions in several prisons, the author's illnesses and other preoccupations, many fellow prisoners, guards, visitors, their backgrounds and problems. The almost endless procession is a revelation to a man who can no longer shun people. The reader is constantly aware of the narrator's effort to control disorder through art in order to present it effectively, along with a philosophy that may control it in life. Contradictory, hypocritical, having evil as its norm, the existing order is no order at all. Hope lies only in opposing chaos, which may be accomplished through human solidarity aroused by suffering, personal or vicarious.

CHAPTER 4

The Psychologist-Stylist

I N this study I have already offered several points of view
on Graciliano Ramos as an artist and a man. I have indicated
how his work presents the Brazilian life of his time, particularly in
the Northeast that he knew best. His interest lay chiefly in the environment, especially the social milieu and its influence on the individual. Not surprisingly, the individual uppermost in his mind was
himself, expressing the feelings and views that are his themes in
everything that he wrote.

In Graciliano's case the single most important structure that
served as a vehicle for his themes was the narrator or protagonist, a
character who became increasingly more autobiographical during
the course of his career. More than the central figure, the protagonist
is the center of Graciliano's universe in art and perhaps in life. He is
the only fully developed character. Moreover, the secondary ones are
presented by him, and their portraits reveal more about him than
them. The topics and aspects of topics that he thinks, speaks, or
writes about are most significant, but of greater significance is how
he deals with what concerns him. Graciliano's style in creating his
characters and re-creating himself has not yet received more than
passing attention in this study. I shall necessarily deal with this subject more fully as I attempt to explore in greater depth Graciliano's
creativity as a "psychologist."[1]

Somewhat unique among Graciliano's first-person protagonists,
João Valério does not realize that he is writing or narrating the book
now before the reader. He merely tells his story as he lives and plans
it. Giving nothing of his physical appearance and with no significant
past, he interests the reader sufficiently through his thoughts and actions. These are so closely linked with Palmeira dos Indios and its inhabitants, of which he makes some description, that no immediate
lack is felt regarding João Valério's person. The opportunistic young

man first imagines marrying Marta Varejão for the dowry that her foster mother, Dona Engrácia, will provide; then he imagines happiness in an affair with Adrião Teixeira's wife Luísa, which is temporarily realized; finally and cynically, he imagines a comfortable, pleasant marriage with Josefa, Adrião's niece, which will probably take place. Having no great illusions about himself, João Valério is equally honest with the reader, who comes to know him very well, so well that he can easily perceive any trace of dishonesty in him.

Regardless of what the narrator says, it is clear from how he says it that he represents his petit bourgeois class. His normal speech consists of standard, everyday language, with a sprinkling of familiar expressions. Having some education, however, João Valério occasionally uses rather erudite terms. Like Graciliano's other protagonists and Graciliano himself, he prefers the earthy word to its more generally accepted synonym, at times for a special effect, at other times simply because it is his preference. Note the violent sensuality expressed for Luísa in the following passage:

Soltei-lhe as mãos, agarrei-lhe a cabeça, beijei-a na bôca, devagar e com voracidade. Apertei-a, machucando-lhe os peitos, mordendo-lhe os beiços e a língua.

I released her hands, grasped her by the head, kissed her on the mouth, slowly, voraciously. I squeezed her, crushing her breasts, biting her lips and tongue.[2]

His entirely dispassionate appraisal of Marta Varejão shows the protagonist's (and the author's) inclination generally to plain language:

Realmente não era feia, com aquêle rostinho morena, grandes olhos prêtos, bôca vermelha de beiços carnudos, cabelos tenebrosos, mãos de mulher que vive a rezar. E alta, airosa, simpática, sim senhor, ótima fêmea. Se ela me quisesse, eu não tinha razão para considerar-me infeliz. (C, 53)

Actually she was not ugly, with that dusky little face, big black eyes, red mouth with fleshy lips, dark hair, the hands of a woman who prays constantly. And tall, graceful, charming, yes indeed, an excellent female. If she wanted me, I had no reason to consider myself unfortunate.

His choice of vocabulary is always appropriate to the character, and plausible for his station and region. Possessed of certain intellectual qualities, he is able to analyze himself and others quite shrewdly, often with reference to modes of expression. Here is a typical brief analysis that begins with a short description of Luísa and concludes with a generalization applicable to the people of the Northeast:

> Diante das visitas, era reservada: não ia além de uma ou outra frase risonha lançada na conversação. Em família, tornava-se expansiva. É o que se observa entre as senhoras do Nordeste. Como os homens aqui são indelicados e não raro brutais, elas se esquivam, tímidas. (C, 76)

> In the presence of guests, she was reserved: she did not go beyond contributing an occasional cheerful remark to the conversation. With the family, she became expansive. This is characteristic of the ladies of the Northeast. As the men here are indelicate and often brutal, they keep themselves aloof because of timidity.

Crude terms and insults such as "idiot" and "scum," sometimes approaching the obscene, are frequent in the mouth of João Valério, whether uttered in anger or through habit. Graciliano and his creatures are extremely severe with their fellows and themselves.

Key words recur that stress certain critical and philosophical attitudes. The word "useless" is applied repeatedly to all spheres of life, from the relatively trivial to the most important, and includes the self. The statue of a bird is made animate and personified. Not only is the statue's raised leg useless, but also its mute advice which goes unnoticed by the protagonist:

> . . . E a garça de bronze, à beira da água, levantava a perna inútil com displicência, mostrava-me o bico num conselho mudo, que não percebi. (C, 80)

> . . . And the bronze heron, at the edge of the water, raised its useless leg with irritation, pointing its beak in my direction with mute advice, which I did not notice.

Drawing analogies between a passage from the Old Testament that speaks of the bitterness of woman as greater than that of death and his current situation vis-à-vis Luísa, the protagonist reflects:

> E a minha tristeza aumentou, porque a rêde em que por muito tempo me debati deixara fugir a prêsa por entre as malhas. E as cadeias, que desejei arrastar, tinham-se afrouxado de repente, abandonando-me, livre e inútil, . . . (C, 143)

And my sorrow increased, because the net in which I struggled for so long had allowed the catch to escape through its threads. And the chains, which I longed to drag, had suddenly been loosed, leaving me free and useless.

Along with precision in vocabulary, Graciliano strove for conciseness in syntax and composition, always seeking maximum effectiveness with maximum economy. He had plenty of occasion to be influenced by the journalistic and commercial styles that have made their weight felt in modern literature. Chapter 24 shows João Valério equally preoccupied with his love affair and efforts to write in several genres, including the journalistic:

A noite passava tempo sem fim sentado à banca, tentando macular a virgindade de uma tira para o jornal de Padre Atanásio. Impotência. . . .
Dançavam-me na cabeça imagens indecisas. Palavras desirmanadas, vazias, cantavam-me aos ouvidos. Eu procurava coordená-las, darhes forma aceitável, extrair delas uma idéia. Nada. (C, 185)

In the evening I spent endless hours seated at the desk, attempting to stain the virginity of a sheet of paper for Father Atanásio's newspaper. Impotence. . . .
Vague images danced in my head. Unrelated, empty words sang in my ears. I was trying to coordinate them, give them acceptable form, extract some idea from them. Nothing.

Caetés already shows Graciliano's constant tendency to combat pompous verbiage and the types behind it by criticism and good example. The verbiage may be literary or professional in nature, as in the case of Dr. Liberato:

Vendo Adrião estirado, a gente perguntava:
— Há perigo, Doutor?
E o Dr. Liberato falava no ventrículo, na aurícula, nas válvulas, e opinava:
— Se não sobrevierem complicações, julgo que não há perigo.
Não sobrevinham complicações. A aurícula, o ventrículo, as válvulas, continuavam a funcionar — e Adrião, combalido, existia. (C, 184)

Seeing Adrião stretched out, people would ask, "Is there any danger, Doctor?"
And Dr. Liberato would speak of the ventricle, the auricle, the valves, and opined, "If no complications arise, I believe there is no danger."
No complications would arise. The auricle, the ventricle, the valves continued to function — and Adrião, an invalid, existed.

More important, Graciliano illustrates through João Valério several types of lucid, compact writing that became distinctive patterns in his work. There is the model of the series of actions, often consisting of little more than three or four verbs, of which I have already given an example above. The series, whether of verbs or other parts of speech, may be staccato and rapid, marking a tense or difficult situation. It may even be epigrammatic, especially when portraying secondary figures. The following illustrates the two preceding types of series simultaneously:

E a D. Maria José, que um dia achou inocentemente que eu era feliz, retorqui de um fôlego, com dureza:
— Feliz por que, D. Maria? Que é que a senhora quer dizer?
Ela espantou-se. Queria sòmente dizer o que tinha dito, mas se eu sentia prazer em ser infeliz, estava acabado, pedia desculpa. O italiano riu, Isidoro encolheu os ombros, o Dr. Liberato fêz uma careta e decidiu:
— Você, meu caro, não está regulando. Vou examiná-lo amanhã. (C, 187)

And to D. Maria José, who one day innocently found me to be fortunate, I replied severely, in a sudden outburst, "Why fortunate, D. Maria? What do you mean?"
She was startled. She meant only what she had said, but if I took pleasure in being unfortunate, that was that, and she begged my pardon. The Italian laughed, Isidoro shrugged his shoulders, and Dr. Liberato made a face and decided, "You, my dear fellow, are not making sense. I'm going to examine you tomorrow."

The next example is more epithetical than epigrammatic, but otherwise fits the pattern for brief descriptions of minor characters:

O Silvério, baixinho, cabeçudo, escovou o pano verde, limpou a tabela, trouxe as bolas e giz. (C, 188)

Silvério, very short, with a big head, swept the green felt, cleaned the edge of the billiard table, brought the balls and chalk.

Rather than drama or characterization, a slower-paced, though always laconic, series may indicate a desire to fix some serious points for the reader's consideration. Such is the case in the example cited above where João Valério attempts to collect his thoughts for an article. His short, objective descriptions of the background noises reinforce the inner disorder conveyed in intellectual rather than emotional terms:

Cães ladrando ao longe, galos nos quintais, gatos no telhado, serenatas na rua, o nordeste furioso a soprar, sacudindo as janelas. (C, 185)

Dogs barking in the distance, roosters in the courtyards, cats on the roof, serenades in the street, the Northeast wind blowing furiously, rattling the windows.

As may be noted in the examples already cited, extreme brevity is often found in a one-word modifier, most commonly exclamatory, frequently negative, ironic or cynical, on the thought previously expressed. Numerous fragmented arrangements, seeming deformations yet permissible within the bounds of good colloquial Brazilian Portuguese, are employed to place unexpected emphasis on or prolong desired elements. For all their "rustic" simplicity, such antithesis and juxtaposition remind the reader of the Classical-Baroque tradition more than of Modernism. Contrary to what occurs in much modern and contemporary writing, once the reader becomes aware that he is dealing with patterns based on natural thought and speech, certain cryptic qualities and ambiguities readily disappear.

The secondary characters of *Caetés* are, of course, introduced and developed through the narrator. João Valério does not furnish the reader complete portraits, but as is natural adds details whenever he encounters his fellow citizens. His observations are a mixture of objective description and personal commentary, as may be seen from the examples given above. With respect to the other principals of the love triangle besides himself, João Valério gradually makes a contrast between Adrião and Luísa. The husband is old and infirm, preoccupied with remedies for his many ailments, with business, and with chess. João Valério wonders what use this decrepit man, with his head full of figures and chess moves, is. The full stature of this pathetic yet heroic man is not disclosed until later. Luísa not only is beautiful, but endowed with many virtues. These include those that she indeed possesses and those that her would-be lover lends her; João Valério regrets that he cannot imagine more of them for her. The real Luísa remains vague, however, until perhaps the end of the novel, as befits the narrator's relationship to her and the rest of Palmeira dos Indios, and Graciliano's purposes. Despite Luísa's tears at the close of the affair with João Valério, her strength and dignity vis-à-vis the protagonist make his shabbiness all the more apparent. His only saving grace is to know himself for what he is, a worthy representative of his society.

The more minor characters of *Caetés* are encountered in the places regularly frequented by João Valério, chiefly in Adrião's home where weekly soirées are held. The narrator gives them more or less space depending on the importance of their roles in the action. Their distinctive features are presented through portraits involving physical and psychological traits, descriptions of their actions, and transcriptions of their speech.

Of the minor figures, Evaristo Barroca receives the greatest attention, although he plays no part in the triangle. He is most prominent in the bureaucracy of Palmeira dos Indios, however, because of his political power in the state, as well as his wealth and, above all, the university degree on which his position largely rests. Thus he represents everything that João Valério, who detests but envies him, is not. Barroca is a kind of force, somewhat removed from the lives of ordinary citizens; his actions are not observed directly, then, but their effect is felt. He is the typical demagogue of Latin countries, having risen to power through rhetoric and the credulity of the masses rather than serious effort or merit. Despite his ignorance, corruption, and arbitrary acts, perceived only by an alert minority, Barroca maintains his position. Even the minority fawns hypocritically, criticizing him only behind his back. João Valério seems a rare exception, for with all his defects, he is essentially honest. Yet it is bitter for him, as for Graciliano, to accept Barroca's fraudulent success, achieved in their eyes at the expense of more worthy individuals. The degree to which the author has his narrator focus on Barroca's person, activities, and especially his oratory is evidence of their jealousy and disgust.

As the reader views the "gallery of types" so vividly portrayed, he may realize that each type has been captured by only one or two traits, an outstanding physical characteristic or mannerism here, a moral quality there, sometimes picturesque, sometimes ridiculous, but never complete. Isidoro Pinheiro is scarcely distinguishable from the other lower-middle-class boarders at Dona Maria José's, except that he is a good, charitable fellow and João Valério's close companion. He offers sharp contrast to Miranda Nazaré, who calls him a "monster" because of his goodness. Pinheiro has few faults; Nazaré has many petty ones typical of his class. Yet he is superior to the others in the learning that he has acquired from constant reading — although again he is diminished by mocking their ignorance and by his own general frivolity. The few traits selected are unchanging and reinforced by repetition, so that whenever a character reappears the reader expects a certain image, gesture, or attitude. He collaborates with the narrator in re-creating the figure, who then becomes the caricature of a human being.

The style of portraiture is impressionistic, then. Much like the brief, often significant scenes drawn by João Valério during interludes in a given episode or between episodes, individual character sketches seem taken from a pad on which the artist keeps "notes" for a larger work. Apart from the whole of *Caetés*, there are the reunions of João Valério with others in between the narrator's direct monologues to the reader. In scenes where many characters are brought together each partial portrait has its place as an important detail. The viewer then sees the total picture and does not think of any part as incomplete. As I have already had occasion to point out in this study, there are many apparent fragments in Graciliano's writing that take on their full meaning only in a broader context, that of a particular volume or of his entire work.

Paulo Honório is quite conscious of composing a novel. As the subject interests him vitally, he is most selective and careful in synthesizing all elements. The narrator having clearly explained his intentions both as a person and a writer, the reader is not surprised that he adheres to them consistently. He does not report everything of a conversation or an event, but only those parts that he considers useful. He likes only the country and São Bernardo; his references to Viçosa and its inhabitants are rare, then, limited strictly to those that have some bearing on his story. The city is merely a necessary geographical location, seemingly with very few residents, as opposed to Palmeira dos Indios which has its own character somewhat apart from its people. Here it is São Bernardo that has character, the one lent it by its master in his loving though spare descriptions throughout the book. It possesses his character, too, for he creates the description as he created the *fazenda*, in his own image.

Unlike João Valério, Paulo Honório has a physical appearance in addition to his personality and a past, both remote and recent. His age, weight, bushy gray eyebrows, and ruddy, bearded face contribute to the respect that people show him. He is a somber, hard man, displeased with the way that he looks and feeling old at fifty, although his health is good. He considers himself a kind of emotional-cultural cripple, having a small heart, an incomplete brain, a nervous system different from that of other men; not to mention his enormous nose, mouth, and fingers. He blames his rude way of life for the way that he is. It is through his self-portrait and autobiography that the reader learns of Paulo Honório's strength, a strength that he has needed to survive. Unfortunately, it is not only the strong who feel his power. Paulo Honório has nothing but contempt for the weak; his ability to make them suffer gives him a greater sense of security. The narrator remembers his earliest years little, except that he was more or less homeless and worked twelve hours a day as a poorly paid agricultural laborer until the age of eighteen. During the time that he spent in jail for having stabbed a rival in love he learned to read from a Protestant Bible and to do arithmetic to avoid being cheated unduly. His evolution is most pronounced in the recent past and present.

In his style of writing Paulo Honório reveals many of the traits already noted in that of João Valério and, of course, Graciliano. Given his plebeian background in the Northeast, however, Paulo Honório's vocabulary is often coarse as well as regional:

Rosa do Marciano atravessava o riacho. Erguia as saias até a cintura. Depois que passava o lugar mais fundo ia baixando as saias. Alcançava a margem, ficava um instante de pernas abertas, escorrendo água, e saía torcendo-se, com um remeleixo de bunda que era mesmo uma tentação.[3]

Marciano's Rosa was crossing the stream. She held her skirts high about her waist. After she passed the deepest spot she gradually lowered her skirts. As she reached the other side, she remained a moment with her legs spread, dripping water, and got out twisting herself, with a shake of the behind that really was tempting.

Paulo Honório's grammar and syntax are always correct, to be sure, and he is attentive to harmony. The man and the writer are one. A no-nonsense pragmatist, his favorite reading matter is technical in nature. By a series of occupations Paulo Honório has become superior to his acquaintances in wealth and station. Although none of his occupations has prepared him for it, he is superior to them also as a writer. He appears to attribute this slight superiority to his lack of academic training; the kind of learning that he did acquire was not, certainly, to improve him as a man:

. . . Considerando, porém, que os enfeites do meu espírito se reduzem a farrapos de conhecimentos apanhados sem escolha e mal cosidos, devo confessar que a superioridade que me envaidece é bem mesquinha.

Além disso estou certo de que a escrituração mercantil, os manuais de agricultura e pecuária, que forneceram a essência da minha instrução, não

me tornaram melhor que o que eu era quando arrastava a peroba. Pelo
menos naquele tempo não sonhava ser o explorador feroz em que me
transformei. (SB, 247)

. . . Considering, however, that my spiritual adornments are limited to
shreds of knowledge collected at random and poorly sewn together, I must
confess that the superiority of which I boast is quite wretched.

Besides, I am certain that commercial notation and manuals on
agriculture and cattle-raising, which furnished the essence of my instruction,
did not make me better than I was when I was a laborer. At least in those
days I did not dream of being the fierce exploiter that I have become.

Paulo Honório's language reflects his pragmatic taste, although
there is warmth and poetry in it on occasion. The following passage
illustrates, first the protagonist's normally practical view of things
on the *fazenda*, then a more aesthetic view recently suggested by his
wife:

Saí, dirigi-me ao curral, bebi um copo de leite. Conversei um instante com
Marciano sôbre as corujas. Em seguida fui passear no pátio, esperando que
o dia clareasse de todo.

Realmente a mata, enfeitada de paus-d'arco, estava uma beleza. (SB, 227)

I went out, headed to the corral, drank a glass of milk. I chatted for a moment with Marciano about the nighthawks. Then I went for a walk in the
patio, waiting for the sun to get high.

The forest, with the *paus-d'arco* in flower, was really a sight to behold.

The protagonist's affective side is seen especially in descriptions of
São Bernardo, which become more poetic under Madalena's influence. Because she keeps herself in the study to write and does not
enjoy the beauties of the *fazenda*, some of which she has taught him
to appreciate, Paulo Honório refers to his wife in coarse language:

— Em que estará pensando aquela burra? Escrevendo. Que estupidez!
. . . .
A distância arredondava e o sol dourava cocurutos de montes. Pareciam
extraordinárias cabeças de santos.

— Se aquela môsca-morta prestasse e tivesse juízo, estaria aqui
aproveitando esta catervagem de belezas. (SB, 218)

"What can that fool be thinking of? Writing. Such stupidity!"
. . . .
The visibility was increasing all around and the sun was gilding the moun-

taintops. They seemed to be extraordinary saints' heads.
"If that deadhead were any good and had sense, she'd be here taking advantage of this wealth of beauty."

As though to console himself for Madalena's absence, he proceeds to survey the *fazenda* more in the old proprietary, patriarchal manner. Although not devoid of lyricism, Paulo Honório's contemplation here is more epic-heroic.

Paulo Honório's warmth, then, expresses itself in less tender ways as well. Whether they deserve it or not, his inferiors are often treated roughly, with vulgar and even obscene terms (usually censored in the retelling), sometimes in disdain, sometimes in anger. Despite Dona Glória's hard life devoted to Madalena, she has not been successful according to Paulo Honório's materialistic standards, and so he deals with her contemptuously for the most part. Padilha is a miserable, repugnant wretch, whom the master of São Bernardo unmercifully uses as his whipping boy. The depth of Paulo Honório's jealous rage and violence with Madalena may be judged not only by the crudeness of his insults, but that they are repeated in their original form in his memoirs, where he acknowledges her innocence and his grief. Here is part of the scene where the jealous husband discovers a letter supposedly written by his wife to a lover:

Sim senhor! Carta a homem!
Estive um tempão caminhando debaixo das fruteiras.
— Eu sou algum Marciano, bando de filhos das putas?
E voltei furioso, decidido a acabar depressa com aquela infelicidade. Zumbiam-me os ouvidos, dançavam-me listras vermelhas diante dos olhos.
Ia tão cego que bati com as ventas em Madalena, que saía da igreja.
— Meia-volta, gritei segurando-lhe um braço. Temos negócio.
— Ainda? perguntou Madalena.
E deixou-se levar para a escuridão da sacristia. (SB, 220)

"Yes, sir! A letter to a man!"
I continued to walk under the fruit trees for a long while.
"Am I some kind of Marciano, sons of bitches?"
And I returned furious, determined to put a speedy end to that misfortune. My ears were buzzing, red flashes danced before my eyes.
I went so blindly that I bumped Madalena with my nose as she was leaving the church.
"Turn right around," I shouted, holding her by the arm. "We have some business."
"Still?" asked Madalena.
And she allowed herself to be led into the darkness of the sacristy.

Again there are key words that emphasize attitudes and themes. The adjective "enormous" is frequent, either in reference to the size of objects or to their grossness and the disgust of the viewer. Similarly, "little" recurs to designate things or people that are small or insignificant in some way. I have already noted how the protagonist applies these adjectives to himself, "enormous" for those parts that have nothing to do with sensitivity or intellect, "little" for those that do. This passage is a most representative one:

> Foi êsse modo de vida que me inutilizou. Sou um aleijado. Devo ter um coração miúdo, lacunas no cérebro, nervos diferentes dos nervos dos outros homens. E um nariz enorme, uma bôca enorme, dedos enormes. (SB, 250)

> It was this way of life that made me useless. I am a cripple. I must have a small heart, lapses in my brain, nerves different from the nerves of other men. And an enormous nose, an enormous mouth, enormous fingers.

His rare moments of satisfaction or admiration are expressed by "decent," "reasonable," and, very rarely, "excellent," which are Graciliano's key words for such experiences. Paulo Honório often considers the futility of life, however, and the attributes "deception" and "useless" are repeated as in the other works of Graciliano.

Above all, the narrator's material is well chosen and well organized, in spite of his criticism to the contrary. Here again the synthesizing influences operating on Graciliano and Paulo Honório and their own inclinations are evident. The result is more of the same clear, laconic style in the designs discussed above. Particularly common is the reader's impression of having a diary before him; but he recalls at the same time that the notes derive from recollections which, however vivid, are generally of events that date from five years earlier. For all Paulo Honório's apparent objectivity, which he strives to maintain, the material is twice distilled, once by his state of mind in the past and a second time by his present state plus the consciousness of an artist.

Paulo Honório's chief reason for writing his memoirs is to escape his present life of regrets by retracing his past in order to understand it, lay it to rest, and perhaps proceed from there. Madalena plays an important role in both time zones, and her portrait is sketched by her husband as he tries to fix her memory. Her physical and psychological makeup crystallizes gradually through passing references by Paulo Honório, who also reports those of others. The reader's impression is always that of a gentle, refined, high-minded person.

After Paulo Honório, Madalena evolves the most. Unlike her aunt, she has not been crushed by their struggle against poverty to achieve respectability. Whereas Dona Glória alternates in an undignified manner between arrogance, based on a status now lost, and humility, Madalena has been tempered by hardship and education. The master of São Bernardo may destroy her idealism and desire to live, but not her dignity. Madalena owes her spirituality at least partially to death and a certain idealization by her remorseful husband. He seems to find it necessary from time to time to summarize her virtues, as though to emphasize to himself and the reader the effect that she has had on him.

The roles of other lesser characters in the narrative are determined equally by Paulo Honório's view of them. Many are no more than background figures. Some, serving merely to bolster the protagonist's self-importance, are always presented in humiliating postures and circumstances. Paulo Honório dwells on Padilha's rotten teeth and other aspects of his physical appearance, for example, making them represent his moral decadence. Although Graciliano's satirical intention in creating such stable figures is far less than in *Caetés*, their predictability and the narrator's affect the reader in much the same way. Occasionally, Paulo Honório considers one of these with a degree of sympathy, such as the good-natured brute Casimiro Lopes, but only if he is a henchman or otherwise an extension of the master.

While he has nothing but scorn for those who are ashamed of their reversals, Paulo Honório seems inclined to pity those who accept tragedy philosophically, as he himself is now doing. Madalena's is a special case, to be sure. The "excellent" Seu Ribeiro is another one, however, who for the same reason receives special treatment. In fact, the narrator interrupts his first-person account to record Ribeiro's whole story as he received it. The first part describes what used to be in the happy past; the second narrates a series of events in Ribeiro's socioeconomic decline because of his inability to adapt to changing times. The changes are those that have permitted Paulo Honório to become master of São Bernardo, while Seu Ribeiro has accepted a position as bookkeeper with him. Yet Ribeiro retains his dignity in the face of adversity, as Madalena did, as Paulo Honório will, but as Dona Glória generally cannot. No doubt Seu Ribeiro's life serves Paulo Honório as a model when he and others desert São Bernardo after Madalena's death, and the master begins to lose every material possession as well as the few human attachments that he has made.

Like Paulo Honório, Luís da Silva tells his story by way of catharsis. The protagonist of *Angústia* has always been introspective,
however, as well as solitary. Seriously troubled, too, now
recuperating from a long delirium, Luís produces a narrative even
more intimate than *São Bernardo. Angústia* is a long, detailed interior monologue resembling the confession that a patient makes to
his psychiatrist. As in the two previous novels, there is a love triangle
in which the narrator participates, and it is from his perspective that
all characters and events are presented. The basic plot is complicated
by Luís' attempted analysis of the several periods and states of mind
in his past leading to the neurosis, crime, and madness. Much of its
explanation lies in the remote past, but the main action occurs in the
past also; only the narration occupies the present. In order to understand the narrator's confusion and relate lucidly what he relates con-
fusedly, it is important for the reader to keep separate the different
levels of the past, each with its events and characters. When Luís
starts his story he is thirty-five and lives in Maceió, Alagoas, where
he is a government employee and journalist of little consequence.
There is some mystery about him, but gradually, as he responds to
stimuli from the surroundings, the obscurity is dispelled. Places, people, and events of Luís' childhood and youth crowd in on him in the
recent past, which is the present time of the narrative.

From all levels, in the piecemeal fashion familiar to the reader of
Graciliano's impressionistic style, Luís' physical appearance
emerges. His mirror tells him that he is ugly, with dull eyes, a wide
mouth, and a big nose. Physically, he views himself as gross; psychologically, he is insignificant:

> Que iria fazer por aí, miúdo, tão miúdo, que ninguém via?

> What could I do there, small, so small that no one would see me?[4]

After his crime, as a result of illness, Luís is extremely nervous and
his hands shake:

> Vivo agitado, cheio de terrores, uma tremura nas nãos, que emagreceram.
> (A, 5)

> I am always nervous, full of fears, with trembling hands that have grown
> thin.

Again he looks in the mirror, and he has grown thin, feeble, old, the
color of dried earth. The following illustrates Luís' customary view

of himself, as well as the typically dry, seemingly disjointed style of Graciliano's protagonists:

Olhei os dedos com atenção, cheirei-os. Fedor de azinhavre, terra nas unhas. Porcaria. (A, 123)

I looked at my fingers attentively, smelled them. A moldy stench, dirty fingernails. Disgusting.

During the whole novel the narrator provides information concerning his psychology and moral qualities, either directly or indirectly. Luís often compares his poor, unkempt clothes with Julião Tavares' elegant attire. He is careless, unable to concentrate, suffers from feelings of inferiority. These originate in his childhood and are reinforced throughout his wretched existence. Luís has had little experience with women, who intimidate him easily. Daydreams are a good escape for him; although he would like to assert himself, he is too weak-willed.

It is clear that Luís' repression and frustration will erupt in violence under the right conditions, to which Julião Tavares contributes increasingly. At the outset Luís finds Tavares irritating because their ways of thinking, and especially their modes of expression, are so different. The latter is one of the many university-educated individuals in Graciliano's work, and in life, whose rhetoric masks lack of intellectual content and originality. In his presence Luís can no longer give vent to his spleen regarding authors of the same type, for Tavares is there to praise them now. The protagonist begins to hate Tavares, at first suggesting his death by saying that his voice must be stilled, later declaring plainly that his death is necessary. Eliminating Tavares becomes an obsession, which Luís recognizes as such, recognizing also that, for the moment at least, it makes him a different man, more important, fearless, happy.

Although Luís da Silva's views on style closely parallel those of his creator and fellow narrators, he has had some formal education and done considerable reading and writing. Despite *sertanejo* regionalisms, then, particularly in those sequences that recall his childhood, his language is richer than João Valério's and certainly Paulo Honório's. Its greater syntactical complexity is explained, too, by a confused state of mind. Yet the protagonist speaks in effective fragments also when he wishes to be emphatic or to underscore tension. This style is especially noticeable as he approaches the climax where he puts an end to his inner struggle by a violent act. In general very timid outwardly, in his intimate confession Luís expresses himself forcefully regarding his fellows, in terms as pejorative as those that he often applies to himself:

Alguns rapazes vêm consultar-me:
— Fulano é bom escritor, Luís?
Quando não conheço fulano, respondo sempre:
— É uma bêsta. (A, 43)

Some fellows come to consult me, "Is So-and-So a good writer, Luís?" When I do not know So-and-So, I always answer, "He's an idiot."

He is hard on those who make their way without merit on the strength of a university degree, or through socioeconomic or political influences. For all their position they are "idiots," "illiterate," and "scum."

The protagonist seems hardest on the girl who, although he pretends otherwise at first, arouses him sexually, calling Marina "stupid," "affected," "tramp," and worse as the action progresses. At the same time Luís does not distinguish her overmuch from the many other things and people that make his life miserable. The following examples represent the curve that his attitude takes regarding Marina:

E o pessoal se calava, arregalava os olhos para Marina, que não ligava importância a ninguém, ia fôfa, com o vestido colado às nádegas, as unhas vermelhas, os beiços vermelhos, as sobrancelhas arrancadas a pinça. (A, 93)

And people stopped talking, staring at Marina, who paid no attention to anyone and kept moving, all soft, her dress stuck to her buttocks, her nails red, her lips red, her eyebrows plucked.

Aquêles modos pudicos, aquêles movimentos quase imperceptíveis das pálpebras roxas que velavam olhos inúteis, irritaram-me. (A, 171)

Those modest ways, those almost imperceptible movements of her purplish-red eyelids shading useless eyes, irritated me.

Os sapatos velhos, rachados e cambados. A roupa desfiando-se nas costuras. Tão miúda, tão reles. (A, 170)

Her old shoes, cracked and turned down. Her clothes coming apart at the seams. So slight, so wretched.

Apart from plebeian influences and unhappiness, both characteristic of Graciliano and his protagonists, Luís' growing use of coarse language marks a kind of regression, which in this case is a symptom of illness and in others of different unfortunate conditions.

An additional key to Luís' mental state is his preoccupation with grease and impurity, focused on fat, sweaty individuals such as Tavares whose prosperity and rhetoric are suspect, as well as on his own shortcomings. The adjectives "fat," "oily," and the like are used more often and with more connotations by Luís than by any other character of Graciliano's. Here are some examples, all describing Tavares:

> Julião Tavares sorria e continuava a derramar a voz azeitada. (A, 74)

> Julião Tavares smiled and continued to pour out his oily voice.

> Um sujeito gordo, suado, vermelho, bem falante, de olhos abotoados. (A, 88)

> A fat fellow, sweaty, red, a talker, with buttoned-up eyes.

> As palavras gordas iam comigo. (A, 91)

> The unctuous words followed me.

Among Graciliano's favorite words the narrator of *Angústia* employs also "enormous" and "little" still more. The recurring memory of his father's enormous feet as he lay dead strangely excites him; he is overwhelmed by enormous guffaws and books at the office, an enormous fan open on a girl's thighs, and in his delirium by a belly on the wall growing ever more enormous. On the other hand, Luís feels everything about himself and others like him to be very small, insignificant, and helpless. Above all, everything strikes him as "useless."

As in the other novels, the narrator gradually draws portraits of the minor figures by means of brief, partial descriptions and reports of their actions. Julião Tavares is, of course, a most important secondary character in *Angústia*. In addition to the attributes given to him by Luís that I have already mentioned, Tavares' abundant speech is emphasized, in direct dialogue and especially in the protagonist's comments. In profusion, unctuousness, and superficiality, Tavares' way of speaking reflects his whole despicable person and character. Marina, the other important member of what comes to be a love triangle, appears initially in an impressionistic series of physical elements spied by Luís in the next courtyard. He tries to concentrate on his book, but notices bright yellow hair, painted red lips and fingernails, a flash of bare leg. Upon closer acquaintance, Luís learns that the inner Marina is as superficial and frivolous as her outward appearance suggests. Often he recalls and transcribes her conversation in dialogue form to demonstrate ignorance and lack of manners. Luís summarizes the Marina that he "constructed" over the months of their courtship, as he now reconstructs her from memory. The narrator admits that, considered in isolation, what he once took as defects in her he now accepts as components without which Marina would not be Marina. Moreover, she was soft and very clean. She undergoes several physical and psychological transformations, as I have noted above, from Luís' extravagant sweetheart to Tavares' haughty mistress and, finally, to the fallen woman who must have an abortion. Marina and her equally guilty mother attribute their shame to blind fate, but Luís understands what the real forces are whose instruments they have all been. Desperate, seeing no way to combat these forces — there is no faith in the revolution preached by Moisés because the latter is a coward — he decides to seek vengeance on the least sympathetic of the instruments.

Immediately avenged are the poor wretches deftly captured by Luís' brush strokes who live in anguish about him: Moisés, the would-be revolutionary, Pimentel, an unhappy newspaperman, Seu Ivo, a miserable begger, and Vitória, Luís' slow-witted maid. Here, by way of illustration, is a passage concerning the latter:

— Vá descansar, Vitória.
Conselho inútil. O céu de Vitória, miudinho, onde grilos e formigas moravam, tinha sido violado. (A, 124)

"Go rest, Vitória."
Useless advice. Vitória's heaven, a bit of a place, where crickets and ants lived, had been violated.

With Seu Ramalho, Dona Adélia, and their daughter, Marina, the sudden hero has other neighbors who lead similarly unsuccessful, sordid, hopeless existences. Luís' past, too, contains parallels of these Naturalistic victims: Dona Aurora and others from the boardinghouse where he lived as a student: and before them, his father and grandfather, their *vaqueiros* (cowboys), and others on the *fazenda*. I have had occasion to discuss how *Angústia* already represents the author's autobiography and subsumes the milieux and characters of his fiction as well. Julião Tavares is the scapegoat for much of the injustice suffered by many in Graciliano's works.

Such characterization as takes place in *Vidas Sêcas* is accomplished by the third person, either of the omniscient author or in direct monologue. I have already noted how, on the one hand, Graciliano's penetration of his characters is so complete that the reader scarcely perceives the use of the third person. On the other hand, even when they address themselves mentally — they communicate very little verbally, often using no more than grunts or gestures with one another — Fabiano and his family employ the third person. Perspectives converge, then, to objectivize the characters, not so much to dehumanize them as to make them representative of a class. They have been dehumanized, to be sure, but by their environment and society rather than by Graciliano. Nor does lack of individualization here reflect the author's insensitivity or a purely intellectual attitude. On the contrary, although the characters have been reduced by conditions almost to the status of objects or animals, and by the novelist to that of symbols, they are presented with the greatest of sympathy for their plight.

It is the highest tribute to Graciliano that he evokes similar compassion in the reader without offering him any but the most general notions of the characters' physical appearance, costume, or home. Fabiano, Vitória, and their sons could be anyone of the *vaqueiro* class in the Northeast. Indeed, Fabiano's sons remain nameless, designated merely as the "older" and the "younger." The dog Baleia is named and personified, however, perhaps because animals play at least as important a role in the region as the humans whose fortunes they share. Note the human qualities of the dog who is about to die:

Baleia queria dormir. Acordaria feliz, num mundo cheio de preás. E lamberia as mãos de Fabiano, um Fabiano enorme. As crianças se espojariam com ela, rolariam com ela num pátio enorme, num chiqueiro enorme. O mundo ficaria todo cheio de preás, enormes.

Baleia wanted to sleep. She would wake up happy, in a world full of cavies. And she would lick Fabiano's hands, an enormous Fabiano. The children would play with her on the ground, roll with her in an enormous patio, an enormous pen. The world would always be full of cavies, enormous ones.[5]

There is no need to describe these people or their belongings, for everyone knows what little they are and what little they possess. The following passage describes the home that will be theirs for a while, the typically bare, transient home of the *vaqueiro*:

> Estavam no pátio de uma fazenda sem vida. O curral deserto, o chiqueiro das cabras arruinado e também deserto, a casa do vaqueiro fechada, tudo anunciava abandono. Certamente o gado se finara e os moradores tinham fugido. (VS, 12 - 13)

> They were in the patio of a lifeless *fazenda*. The deserted corral, the goat pen in ruins and equally deserted, the *vaqueiro's* house shut up, everything indicated abandonment. Certainly the cattle had died and the tenants had fled.

The characters themselves are aware of their poverty and virtual anonymity as *sertanejos*. *Vidas Sêcas* is an allegory of life in the *sertão* with Fabiano and his family as Everyman.

Consistent with the nature of allegory, *Vidas Sêcas* develops general psychological and moral qualities, personifying them through its characters. Graciliano's narration of their actions and record of their very sparse dialogue, and especially their thoughts, skillfully portray the ignorance and poverty of the *sertanejo*. Given these conditions, he cannot but be naïve, both trusting and wary, and perservering, although resigned to suffering. Not only his behavior but the space devoted to each member of Fabiano's family befit his station and importance in the regional culture. Vitória, although more astute than Fabiano, is appropriately concerned with domestic matters and subject to her husband. He is attentive to her wishes, but his role is the most dominant in the novel as in the patriarchal society depicted. The younger son is of an age to be thinking of what he will be; quite naturally, he expects to be a *vaqueiro*. The older one is still at a stage where certain forbidden words puzzle and fascinate him. Yet both are beginning to acquire the walk become "hereditary" among *vaqueiros* who spend most of their lives on horseback rescuing cattle lost in the thorny *catinga*. Long-suffering, devoted to the end to duty and her masters, dreaming only of enough to eat, even if it is not in this life, Baleia represents all of them. The author makes the identification in Fabiano's mind clear:

> Êles velhinhos, acabando-se como uns cachorros inúteis, acabando-se como Baleia. (VS, 154)

They would be little old people, ending their days like useless dogs, ending their days like Baleia.

The memory of a faithful bitch that his family had to destroy, used in *Angústia* as in the story that became a chapter of *Vidas Sêcas*, seems to have impressed Graciliano as a good symbol of his oppressed people.

The technique of the third person in *Vidas Sêcas*, with dialogue reduced to the smallest amount in any of Graciliano's novels, makes for still more standardized language than in the three preceding works. Virtually free of slang and vulgar terms, *Vidas Sêcas* nevertheless abounds in regionalisms. Yet these are not intended to be esoteric in nature or picturesque in effect. Most common are those regionalisms of the Northeast widely known in Brazil and already familiar in Graciliano's lexicon. The expression is simple as well as colloquial, for Fabiano and his fellows are suspicious of "difficult" words, generally used to cheat them:

> Ouvira falar em juros e em prazos. Isto lhe dera uma impressão bastante penosa: sempre que os homens sabidos lhe diziam palavras difíceis, êle saía logrado. (VS, 118)

> He had heard of interest and installments. This had made a rather painful impression on him: every time educated men used difficult words with him, he ended up cheated.

He employs harsh names for enemies, but only to himself and sparingly:

> Ora, o soldado amarelo. . . . Sim havia um amarelo, criatura desgraçada que êle, Fabiano, desmancharia com um tabefe. Não tinha desmanchado por causa dos homens que mandavam. Cuspiu, com desprêzo:
> Safado, mofino, escarro de gente. (VS, 37 - 38)

> Now, the yellow soldier. . . . Yes, there was a yellow one, a miserable creature that he, Fabiano, could take care of with one blow. He had not taken care of him because of the men in authority. He spit, in disgust:
> No-good, rotten, scum of a fellow.

The extreme conciseness of the author's style as a whole here fits his stark, rustic subject equally well. Here is a scene of the effects of the drought:

. . . Encolhido no banco do copiar, Fabiano espiava a catinga amarela, onde as fôlhas sêcas se pulverizavam, trituradas pelos redemoinhos, e os garranchos se torciam, negros, torrados. No céu azul as últimas arribações tinham desaparecido. (VS, 143)

. . . Huddled on the porch bench, Fabiano spied the yellow *catinga*, where the dry leaves were becoming pulverized, crumbled by the gusts of wind, and the gnarled branches were twisted, black, charred. In the blue sky the last migrating birds had disappeared.

Little description is required for the *sertão* and its inhabitants; when necessary, it is provided, often kaleidoscopically as elsewhere in Graciliano's work, as in the town setting given by a presentation of the activities of residents performed simultaneously.

A feira se desmanchava; escurecia; o homem da iluminação, trepando numa escada, acendia os lampiões. A estrêla papa-ceia branqueou por cima da tôrre da igreja; o doutor juiz de direito foi brilhar na porta da farmácia; o cobrador da prefeitura passou coxeando, com talões de recibo debaixo do braço; a carroça de lixo rolou na praça recolhendo cascas de frutas; seu vigário saiu de casa e abriu o guarda-chuva por causa do sereno; sinha Rita louceira retirou-se. (VS, 36)

The market was breaking up; it was getting dark; the lamplighter, climbing a ladder, was lighting the lamps. The evening star grew white over the church tower; his Honor the Judge went to show off in the doorway of the drugstore; the cashier at the Prefecture limped by, a pile of receipt stubs under his arm; the garbage wagon rolled over the square collecting fruit peels; the Reverend Vicar left his house and opened his umbrella because of the dew; Miss Rita, the pottery vendor, closed shop.

In partial compensation for lack of dialogue, many brief, precise, often lapidary narrative series synthesize the characters' elemental actions and thoughts. Nothing is superfluous in this most carefully wrought work composed of patterns in which the author has already exercised and will continue to exercise himself considerably.

CHAPTER 5

The Man and the Humanist[1]

I N preceding chapters I have attempted from different points of view to show structural and linguistic devices developed by Graciliano Ramos to both disguise and reveal himself. Despite a certain natural desire for disguise, his experimentation with several forms of expression seemed to confirm that the need to reveal himself and his ideas with respect to the human condition was stronger. More than ever before, this necessity led him to reduce some of the requisites of fictional art to a minimum, so that he might express himself in the most direct manner possible. Never very important to Graciliano, artistic invention in plot and elements of structure are all but abandoned in *Infância* and the *Memórias do Cárcere.*

This is not to say that the directions his life took are followed in the strict, linear fashion of his first two novels in these works. Graciliano uses the loosest of chronologies as a framework, much as in *Angústia,* shaping according to his purposes only those episodes that his wishes and intelligence dictate. It may be that in *Infância* considerable passage of time clouds the writer's memory, so that greater artifice becomes necessary. Thus, the result is novelistic as well as autobiographical. Characterizing a narrator who is more than the author remains a problem, for he is ostensibly the author as a child. The content, whether regarding himself, "secondary characters," events or circumstances, should be presented from that perspective with those physical, psychological, and linguistic features required to make the protagonist plausible. I have pointed out also how, in addition to autobiography, *Infância* appears often as propaganda, political or simply philosophical. As in the novels, then, behind the narrator clearly stands the author.

The *Memórias* seem much freer of such constraints and far more objective. Yet the reader is warned, not only that the author deals in memories, but that he selects, orders, and emphasizes them as he sees fit. The narrator and author are unquestionably one. Some years have elapsed, to be sure, but Graciliano is an adult in both past and present. There is no need for special separate characterization, linguistic or other. Although he shares a number of features with the protagonists of his novels, he does not have the single overriding problem typical of them that colors their perspective. His view of others is more objective, therefore, but from long practice his manner of presenting the "secondary characters," like his style in general, does not differ substantially from theirs. Contrary to the situation in *Infância,* it is not difficult to say whether fiction or autobiography has the upper hand here.

Nevertheless, Graciliano's purpose in the *Memórias,* more than in any other work, is that of the human being who is also a humanist: to know himself and, through self-knowledge, to know man; and to share his findings with other men. Again, it appears that in the memorialist's philosophy man is subject to conflicting forces. In order to control the chaos and his destruction, he can only exercise his will or intellect. Undisputed triumph is unlikely, however, for the inherent weakness of man and evils of established society thwart any attempt to impose a constructive order. Graciliano the man is surprised and suspicious when real-life individuals are generous or heroic, and especially when they act in concert for the general good. He does not expect men to be either good or bad, but for them to act against their own or class interests seems utterly incomprehensible. When Captain Lôbo insistently offers Graciliano a loan, the latter is astounded at this last favor to him and betrayal of capitalism. The author cannot understand the contradiction on the personal level either, for he has been antagonistic to the Captain despite his liking for him. Feeling trapped in several ways, Graciliano refuses the much needed money. The humanist can seldom accept his fellows' selflessness except in artistic, philosophical, or ideological terms. *Viagem,* the record of Graciliano's trip to the U.S.S.R. after he joined the Communist party, shows that his hope in such acceptance was probably vain.

The first chapter of the four-volume *Memórias* serves as a preface. Graciliano explains why for ten years he has kept silent on the subject of his incarceration, and why now he has decided to break his silence. Not having retained the notes taken in prison, and with the passage of time, he felt it too difficult a task to write of that trying period in his life and in Brazilian history. He hoped that someone

more able might undertake it. Further, Graciliano was most reluctant to deal with living beings undisguisedly, yet did not wish to
make a novel of their experiences. He cannot blame the authorities
for his inertia. Although it is true that some books were burned, censorship as a rule was applied to obviously political writings, affecting
works of art very little. Some men of letters, possibly inept or lazy,
have attributed poor writing to lack of freedom. Graciliano maintains, however, that no one ever enjoys complete liberty. A writer
always has syntax to cope with in the first instance, and social and
political restrictions are chronic. Yet he may work within the
limitations imposed by language and conventions. In fact, despite the
law and censorship, the book stores sell pamphlets attacking the
New Republic, although these sometimes contain praise for men in
power. Authors have not been kept from working, then; they have
merely lost the desire to work.

This irony continues as Graciliano speaks of the well-being of the
spiritual elite, i.e., those in political power, and the conditions of the
wretched materialists, i.e., writers such as himself, who because of
their poverty became scarcely more than spirits. These abandoned
their ambitious literary projects, and to support their families
engaged in proofreading, translation, editing, and various forms of
hack writing. They were demoralized and their standards lowered.
Graciliano alludes to the poor quality of one of his novels, probably
Angústia, offering for now no excuse but bad writing and no opportunity for revision. This idea, sometimes in the form of a direct ac-
cusation of the regime, recurs during his imprisonment, in reference
to *Angústia* and to literature in general, whenever the author thinks
of working.

Graciliano considers why he now feels that circumstances have
changed so that he may write his memoirs. Fortunately, it is not that
he has become indifferent, resembling the fat men of the spiritual
elite. Anyone who ever suffered in prison as he did must remember
and speak out, harshly; life is composed of harsh things. The tran-
quillity that he sometimes believes he has is illusory, for his thoughts
flee from the page. He manages to keep himself working from month
to month, free of the onerous tasks that once were necessary, beginning to emerge from the darkness in which everyone felt as though
dead. Some about whom he wished to be discreet have grown distant
or died. Others have remained close or reappeared, altered by the
years, reviving his already confused recollections. Their urging him
to write his memoirs as a duty convinces him. Graciliano has

attempted to observe them according to their several classes and professions in society and grown to understand, feel, and appreciate them without making hasty judgments. He hopes to offend no one, but does not worry himself. In his physical condition and at the speed with which he writes, he correctly prophesies that his memoirs will very probably be posthumous.

Graciliano explains, too, that he is better qualified for this work than some of his colleagues, who are either too highly specialized in research and analysis or journalists trained in on-the-spot reporting. Having exercised several professions and forgotten all of them, Graciliano has the advantage of complete freedom of method. He may ramble at will, dwelling at length on certain matters, repeating some, barely mentioning others, and skipping still others entirely, regardless of their importance. It may well be an advantage, too, that the author lost his notes. If he still had them, he would feel obliged to consult them constantly to verify all sorts of details. Echoing Boileau now as well as Montaigne, Graciliano states that in any case true things are not always verisimilar. Moreover, what he does not remember without notes cannot be very significant. On the other hand, he may emphasize some particulars to the point of exaggeration. Perhaps he does not tell the exact truth, but neither does he lie. Not only is truth stranger than fiction, then, but relative, dependent on the beholder. Graciliano will not quarrel with others' recollections if they do not quarrel with him about apparent discrepancies.

What is essential is that he has tried always to understand and sympathize with the people about whom he writes, admiring any greatness in them and recognizing his own defects in theirs. He remains sensitive concerning what he may have revealed to them of his most intimate behavior and feelings while in prison. Such self-revelation in person was, as always for the reserved Graciliano, the worst torture inflicted during the year's cohabitation with many different types of humanity under a variety of circumstances, good and bad. He feels it even in the use of the undisguised first person of his narrative, which he justifies as inevitable in such a work. Somewhat ironically, Graciliano promises to minimize his intrusion here as in real life. The reader is, of course, interested primarily in Graciliano and in others only as he presents them.

Several chapters are devoted to the events antecedent to Graciliano's arrest. A politically motivated telephone campaign against him is followed by a request that the author resign his post in the Department of Public Instruction. His immediate superiors have no choice; as is customary in Graciliano's work, the wrongdoers most to blame, whether high or low in station, tend to be anonymous or in the background. In a sense he is relieved to be out of the petty bureaucratic position, but it is normal for him to review possible reasons and persons responsible for his disfavor.

Chiefly his attempts at reform in government and education have made him enemies, but his talk in cafés has been too frank and his novels can be interpreted as revolutionary. To judge by the acquaintances that he meets on the train between Maceió and Recife after his arrest, two out of three are against him. One, a functionary, accuses him of sloppy work, another, a legislator of the wealthy upper class, calls him a Communist, and only the third, now a judge, shows him kindness when ostracism would be more prudent. His desire to find fault with himself, even to deserve imprisonment for some crime, is also properly explained by a need for meaning in a generally cruel, futile existence. In fact, he is a very complex individual. He has a great deal of self-respect, confessing that he watches himself to keep from committing unworthy acts. Graciliano does not always recognize or recall his feelings, but works to clarify them. Here, as in similar instances elsewhere in the *Memórias,* Graciliano doubts that he would have the courage to behave as his benefactor does; and he suffers. In view of the obvious strengths often displayed by Graciliano, physically as well as morally, his suffering seems needless. The author's repeated self-analysis, usually culminating in some self-reproach, may have the ring of false modesty on occasion.

Despite obligations to his wife and children, Graciliano contemplates leaving Alagoas for a fresh start, to write free of any job and free of his nagging, jealous wife. He is not yet aware of the imminence of the desired trip at that point in his recollections. Dona Heloísa does not always receive sympathetic treatment in her husband's memoirs. He does not hesitate to list her defects as he sees them and often seems condescending with regard to her. Yet he appears objective in presenting her, and the reader grows fond of Graciliano's wife, as he must be. For all her faults, she accepts his arrest stoically when it is a fact, doubtless respecting his attitude, because there are outsiders present, and for the sake of the children. Privately with her husband, as when he is about to be taken to Recife, Dona Heloísa weeps in her quiet way, copiously. She is always loyal and helpful, for their sakes and for the children of both marriages. When the author realizes that his departure from home will soon materialize, he is almost pleased. One evening gives him a first taste of what prison does to a man's will. He will have reason to develop this theme throughout the four volumes by his own example and those of fellow inmates ranging from the most courageous to the most frightened. Even when Graciliano is relatively comfortable and calm, his thoughts are as fragmented as the notes that he takes on the spot. Confusion and thoughts of his family keep him from reading, much less concentrating on the book that he thinks to write. Yet he must persist in believing that he will write some book in prison or acquire material for one. Hindsight as such may play a role in the narrative as it does in my commentary.

Having spent the night in unsatisfactory revision of the last pages of *Angústia,* the author receives two fateful visits, as well as some unpleasant telegrams. The first visit is from a disagreeable female relative who berates him for his imprudent behavior; his wife agrees with her. The second is from Luccarini, a former subordinate and one-time enemy at the office, who warns him of his impending arrest and urges him to go into hiding. Graciliano has already made his decision: he prefers the respite afforded by what he believes will be a short stay in prison to what he now endures and would endure as a fugitive. The ensuing quarrel between the author and his wife, as well as justification based on a description of life in hiding, enlist the reader's sympathy for Graciliano's decision. With customary deliberation and calm, he makes his preparations to leave home, bathing, packing, planning.

A third and fourth visit form a parallel of sorts and furnish contrasts with the first two. Dona Irene is a conscientious teacher with whom Graciliano has worked to provide schooling for underprivileged black children in Maceió. In spite of considerable success, described in part by the author, their efforts have not been appreciated by the authorities. Graciliano refers to Dona Irene's hair, turned gray in service, and tries to spare her knowledge of what is about to befall him. His concern for her is touching; it may help to explain Dona Heloísa's jealousy of this kind of woman. The fourth, long-awaited visit is that of the arresting officer. Graciliano recognizes the young mulatto lieutenant as one who on two occasions arrogantly sought special favors for a niece failing in school. While it is unlikely that the lieutenant has been responsible for his misfortune, Graciliano logically wonders how it is that he has the obvious pleasure of taking him off to prison.

These first chapters are carefully arranged but, as always in Graciliano's work, more convincing and moving in the details selected and emphasized than in the larger structure. As the author himself suggests, it matters little if what he composes here rests on historical truth or a re-creation. The scenes as developed by him, or by me as I attempt to summarize and interpret him, are suited to either autobiography or fiction as practiced by Graciliano. Space does not permit extended commentary for the four volumes on such material, however. As Graciliano further suggests, it is the men of whom he writes that constitute the principal matter of this work. It is to them that I shall turn my attention, therefore, as well as to the writer and his conclusions as he views them.

Prior to boarding the train for Recife Graciliano meets Captain Mata, a fellow prisoner who is to be his close companion for some time. A cheerful, talkative man, he presents a striking contrast to the author. In his confused state, the latter does not entirely understand what the Captain says. Graciliano explains that he must make a sorry impression, but the reader understands that Graciliano probably does not have a good first impression of Mata. He will grow accustomed to his companion and fond of him, but Mata remains essentially unchanged. The Captain protests his innocence and that he has been the victim of intrigue, as though Graciliano were his judge. Much to the author's embarrassment, he repeats the protests with every acquaintance of Graciliano's who chances by, unnecessarily calling attention to their situation. During the trip, in conversation resembling a monologue more than dialogue, Mata gives the author his biography. The Captain was a police officer, and considers himself a poet. Having spent some time in Rio professionally, he claims to have distinguished himself by reading his verses at a banquet. For distraction on the hot, dusty train he recites a sonnet, whose satirical intent is at first lost on Graciliano because of its involved language. Whatever the style, superliterary, familiar, or kinetic when speech is inconvenient or forbidden, Mata must communicate with the human beings about him. Graciliano prefers to keep his customary silence, not only speaking but listening as little as possible. He is lost in his thoughts, which are random if not confused, capable of fixing his attention on many things, frequently returning to certain ones, but seldom in a consecutive, sustained manner.

Captain Mata is clearly better suited to the seemingly well-organized, efficient life of a military prison. Graciliano did his military service, spending the few months with no enthusiasm except for gymnastics. Although he later noted that men who had been soldiers worked better, his avowed prejudice continued against the army as costly, useless, and harmful. His current experience, when for example he and Mata are shunted about from one possible lodging to another, until just the type of cell specified in their orders is found, confirms his bias. Graciliano cannot reject, accept, or even understand rigid military symbolism and the set of values that it represents. Mata is materially and psychologically adaptable, sleeping soundly, consuming both his own rations and Graciliano's with relish, and generally seeming to enjoy the life. While he despises the lower middle class, the author is aware that his background in it makes the transition to prison life painful for him. Moreover, he is constantly beset by his chronic sensitivity and feelings of inadequacy.

In addition to the dehumanization of military routine and fear of interrogation, for himself and those that he may betray, Graciliano suffers when a number of assumptions are proven false that he knows to be based on ignorance. Evidently he expects proper discipline and courtesy from officers, and is mortified when he mistakes a well-mannered sergeant for a lieutenant. On the other hand, he is shocked by the triviality of a commandant or the honest brutality of a general. Captain Mata ignores the sergeant, however, and kowtows to the superior officers. Doubtless it is wrong always to expect human beings to follow stereotyped norms, whatever the origins of the stereotypes. Mata accepts the obvious juxtaposition in behavior, chiding the author for his imprudent reaction to that of the general. For all his apparent superficiality, he shows himself to be more realistic than Graciliano. At the same time, like many characters in the *Memórias,* he seems to support another discovery, again admittedly prejudiced, made by the author: the military is well disciplined only on the surface. Its insistence on precise routine is designed to depersonalize the recruit. Once initiated, the latter realizes that what is essential is not to be caught in error, even at the expense of imputing the fault to a comrade. Actually, rules are made to be broken. Thus, military order may disguise many a vice and make the soldier forget moral principles learned in civilian life. Perhaps it is not surprising, too, that Mata finds prison food and other treatment excellent. He becomes apprehensive only when the bugle sounds the arrival of a general, whereas the new environment so profoundly disturbs Graciliano that he experiences almost constant nausea and apathy.

Compared to the formal commandant who encourages hypocrisy, Captain Lôbo is a most sympathetic type. He visits Graciliano and his cellmate daily after the commandant and, although his behavior is usually as predictable as that of any of Graciliano's secondary characters, his speech and gestures lend him greater depth and warmth than is true of others. Lôbo's actions are vigorous, as befit his rank and position, but somewhat abrupt, indicating an inner conflict not exhibited by other prison officers. Exercising control over the captive's person and maintaining discipline are his duty, e.g., seeing to it that each prisoner uses the bath facilities assigned to him according to his station. When he reprimands Graciliano for having broken the rule on this point, the author is surprised that he is not hurt or angry at the scolding. Accustomed from childhood yet sensitive to any criticism, the adult Graciliano would not normally endure such treatment. On the verge of laughter because of the trivial reason for the reprimand, he contains himself when he notes the Captain's sincerity. The prisoner wonders why he is the object of Lôbo's distinction; whether his hopes are not being raised only to be dashed to the ground under harsh conditions later; or if he is presumptuous to assume the operation of anything but chance.

The Captain has no wish, however, to censor or censure thoughts. He may have some notion of Graciliano's ideas as expressed in his writings, yet he never engages him in serious discussion to learn precisely what the prisoner thinks. Repeatedly the reader is reminded that the Captain tells Graciliano he does not agree with his ideas, but that he respects them; and repeatedly Graciliano asks or wonders how this can be if he does not really know them, nor he the Captain's. Lôbo cannot therefore be any more just than the acquaintances encountered by Graciliano on the train. The surprised author appreciates his kindness, which seems genuine, and the principle of tolerance expressed, whether the tolerance is genuine or not. Like Lôbo, the reader may have a relatively clear notion of where the author stands socially and politically from knowledge of his works. Unlike the interrogator, however, the reader is not reluctant to learn more and is privy to a number of brief explanations by Graciliano prompted by recollections of his reactions to the activities of the famous Luiz Carlos Prestes.

The author is disturbed to learn that Prestes has been arrested. Rough *sertanejos* admired the heroism of the leader of the celebrated Column in 1924, but Graciliano considers that it was no more than a protest. If the Column had miraculously succeeded, it would have been disastrous in the conservative backlands. The idea of uniting the scattered primitive Indians is ridiculous, nor would redistributing the land, which of itself does not constitute wealth in the Northeast, serve any useful purpose for the *vaqueiro*. Something needed to be done, but not according to the principles of urban revolutionaries ignorant of the problems of the *sertão*. Graciliano is hopeful that the first attempt at revolution taught some necessary lessons and helped to prepare a more successful second attempt. Although to date he has limited himself to relatively harmless conversations and writing, the author now includes himself in the revolutionary movement. Circumstances sometimes sweep us up and thrust terrible responsibilities on us beyond our capabilities. Despite this realization, Graciliano promises himself to follow a "reasonable" course of action. Held indefinitely without arraignment through the fascistic regime's fear of public opinion, the author can be little more than fate's plaything for the time being. He almost regrets not being a more dangerous type when, on the verge of pressing the well-bred censor to read his wife's letter, he is irritated by the ignominy of the officer's position and his own desire to prove the letter innocent. The censor dismisses him, saying that having him open his mail in his presence is a mere formality. Continuing his analysis after the fact, Graciliano interprets the supposed courtesy as condescension for an inoffensive member of the officer's own class. Lôbo's behavior derives from quite different sentiments that the author cannot always understand. Almost the only action of which Graciliano is capable in prison is taking notes and thinking of an eventual book. In a work such as the *Memórias* he will relate sad cases like that of Nunes Leite, a lawyer completely demoralized because due process no longer has any meaning. In short, nothing offered by any party thus far makes much sense to Graciliano.

Despite his extreme pessimism, however, the author has had and continues to have some good experiences. Often in his reporting he pauses to weigh one event against another and sift his thoughts and afterthoughts on them. In the hold of the *Manaus* he meets all types of prisoners, hardened criminals, religious fanatics, leftist revolutionaries. Among the latter, a large number have been badly tortured, yet their spirits have not been crushed. Graciliano is led to compare attitudes on crime and corporal punishment in the *sertão* as he recalls them from his own severely chastised youth. Murder is not considered serious in the Northeast where death from all sorts of causes is common and life cheap. Thievery on a grand scale, usually perpetrated by the upper classes through more or less legal means, escapes punishment also. Such crimes, over which the ordinary people have no control, are accepted with resignation as are the other evils inherent in the environment. It is the petty thief who suffers cruelly, for the *sertanejo* mind does not attribute his crime to God's will or immutable fate. The degradation of corporal punishment, associated with slaves and others at the very bottom of the social scale, is strongly resisted. One who endures it can never recover his honor, and so prefers death. Graciliano is therefore surprised to learn that the political prisoners, many of them from the middle class, are not ashamed of the treatment they have suffered. They believe in their social reforms and will not permit the authorities, who attempt to degrade them as thieves, to diminish their cause. Further, their ranks are so numerous that they cannot think of themselves as a minority and are comforted; they speak of their physical pain as a commonplace, no more dishonorable than an accident or operation. Their guards and other immediate representatives of the government often feel as they do.

More painful is the irony that makes fellow prisoners inflict torture on one another. Occasionally deliberate, their behavior in this sense is usually involuntary. Unsanitary, crowded conditions and tension are to blame. The young black man lying naked and scratching his scrotum does not intend to irritate the author. Graciliano does not mean to impose repeatedly on the man in the lower bunk for matches. All view with suspicion anyone who looks or acts in any way different. At first Graciliano is taken for a spy because of his formal attire. Soon he is accepted, inexplicably, and the unhappy Van der Linden ostracized, for no better reasons. Similarly, the regular passengers, wittingly or unwittingly supporters of the regime, may cause the prisoners suffering. More with curiosity than hostility, they stare as at freaks in a sideshow. They peer down and throw tangerine skins into the hold as though it were a large cage at the zoo. Still, there is room for some optimism. At worst, the optimism is purely egocentric: by inflicting pain on another, the tormentor realizes some degree of superiority, however wretched he himself may be.

Graciliano often counterbalances a cause for pessimism with a cause for optimism, however, thus showing that a true realist does not necessarily portray life always in somber hues even when it seems to warrant them most. If one guard is extraordinarily brutal, there is another who helps him on several occasions. If tangerine skins falling on his chest disturb Graciliano's rest and make him indignant, their odor is a welcome change from the customary stench in the hold of the ship. If his fellow captives are often a trial to him and to each other, they offer assistance, distraction, and enlightenment also. Frequently they give evidence of great solidarity too, as when the samba artist, Paulo Pinto, leads them in dance that expresses and releases their frustrations. Moreover, the regular passengers, instead of complaining of the noise or protesting the manifestation, participate as spectators and applaud. More concerned about the poor quality of his work than of his health, the author has not thought of suicide. Extreme apathy makes him reject the environment in other self-destructive ways, yet he cannot remain indifferent to his body's reactions in the form of a hemorrhage. He has not completely lost the instinct of self-preservation, not to mention his fastidiousness. These characteristics are perhaps more discernible in the moral sphere than in the physical with Graciliano, as when he steadfastly refuses to name a religion that he does not have, or to give up the iodine needed to treat a minor ailment. At best, there is optimism for survival in the author's repeated observation that, without reminders of liberty, the prisoners soon became accustomed to their lot; and in the admission that he adapts easily to any condition. Yet there is ample evidence to the contrary in the narrator's memory of his reactions past and present, for optimism for survival on a higher level.

The first volume of *Memórias do Cárcere* gives some of the immediate background of Graciliano's arrest and recalls his initiation to prison life. It serves also as the reader's introduction to the specific subject and reminds him of themes, structures, and techniques used elsewhere by the author. The reader has learned, for example, that Graciliano's health, seldom good, has deteriorated, especially as a result of the sea voyage from Recife to Rio in the hold of the *Manaus*. His operation in 1932, a complex and apparently unsuccessful one, has left him with chronic abdominal pains and one crippled leg. These physical problems generally worsen through the successive stages of his incarceration. An inherent fastidiousness, the quality of prison food, and above all a psychosomatic condition often cause Graciliano to fast for long periods. A week or more at a time with no more than a bit of bread and milk, not to mention large quantities of drugged coffee, make him weak and apathetic in every way. Not fully understanding a guard's advice not to drink much of the coffee, Graciliano learns only toward the end of his imprisonment that it contains an anaphrodisiac; although he refuses to drink any more, he believes that drugging the coffee may be an act of charity to prisoners. This is also one of many examples of the author's ambivalence on the question of captivity versus freedom.

Having lived as solitary an existence as possible in the midst of large family situations, Graciliano is not comfortable living in the company of his fellow prisoners. He gets along well enough with most of the people that he encounters; and at times to his dismay, he is usually treated with some consideration, perhaps because of his age and poor health, which makes him appear older, his position in civilian life and in letters, and his generally reasonable behavior. The author even recalls a number of relatively close relationships, with prisoners of all sorts, particularly the few women among the political captives, and with guards also. Yet he feels himself to be a stranger everywhere. As a petit bourgeois he is removed from some of the upper class with whom he plays poker. Their clothing is similar, but they are very different in wealth and manners. Graciliano is equally distant from the worker class because of its tendency to demagoguery and coarseness. He finds a certain cooperation among the classes, as when all contribute to help the starving returnees from the penal colony on the Ilha Grande, but no real solidarity on the individual, human level. This attitude is expressed toward the end of the second volume, at a time in the memoirs when Graciliano's stay in the Rio prison is ending. He has already had some evidence to make him feel less a stranger. As he later admits, however, he is to realize that genuine selflessness does exist, as it probably does in ordinary life, only under the most wretched conditions in the penal colony.

At the beginning of the *Memórias* Graciliano explains that he almost looked forward to going to prison for a respite from the many cares of civilian and domestic life and for the opportunity to write. Although it does not take him long to become aware that he was wrong regarding these matters, he soon acquires a certain sense of security in prison. Correspondingly greater is the degree of insecurity concerning life on the outside that characterizes many prisoners. The author reports and analyzes cases of prisoners who commit new crimes in order to remain in prison, despairing of reintegration into society and fearing persecution by the police. Even the prospect of the transfer to the penal colony at the close of the second volume makes Graciliano write that returning to civilian life would be a greater misfortune. Despite the continuous, eventually successful efforts of his wife and a few friends such as Lins do Rêgo and José Olympio to rehabilitate him as a citizen and promote him as an author, he wonders what he would do. He feels half dead, incapable of working, and concerned about what former acquaintances would think of him.

Graciliano's stay in the penal colony, which occupies most of the third volume, shows him which is the worse misfortune. He learns that most of what he has heard about the place is true. The miserable prisoners are in large part reduced to the level of animals, often brutalized by guards or abused by degenerate criminals. One of several scenes that fix themselves in Graciliano's and the reader's memory is that of one reception given to newcomers to the colony. A deformed, sadistic individual informs them that all of them are equal, none has any rights, and they are not there to be reformed, but to die. The phrase "You have come to die," like similar dramatic phrases, punctuates the author's reactions and meditations on events or situations that strike him. A short acquaintance with the place is enough to dispel any illusion, but to have someone express the purpose of the colony so unequivocally is a shock. The prisoners constitute a large group, some of which do not have any idea of why they are there; yet they do not even have the right to live. Moreover, their death will be a slow, arduous one, yet perhaps not so horrible as the speedier one by torture that many have imagined. Graciliano thinks with irony of the generally mild manners of Brazilians and how, in bad faith or idiocy, some individuals publicize this national tendency. He prefers to believe that a few remain well intentioned, and that all of them are caught in the gears of some awful machinery. The thought of imminent death does not displease him at this point.

Despite dreadful conditions in the penal colony, the horror is not unrelieved. Graciliano again receives somewhat preferential treatment and, although his health grows worse, he is able to read and do a bit of writing. Again his reminiscences permit him to engage in some literary criticism. Along with comments on the attempts of fellow prisoners along the way to write, there are instances of criticism of a few of the leading novelists of the day. The author is hardest on himself and his good friend Lins do Rêgo, complaining that the latter does not limit himself to personal experience, where his work is always excellent. Jorge Amado is the writer who most appeals to the revolutionaries and proletariat in the penal colony. As elsewhere, Graciliano meets some interesting, likable people with whom to share trials and even an occasional moment of humor. Gaúcho, referred to in one of the narratives of *Insônia,* stands out among these. There are a number of guards and soldiers, too, who feel and for whom one feels sympathy. The author witnesses acts of true generosity and heroism, both individual and collective. Now and then Graciliano experiences a certain cowardice or guilt, believing at the same time that everyone's first duty is to survive. Yet he too reveals courage on occasion, sometimes aggressively, and in this there is evidence not only of a desire to live, but to live as a man. When the telegram arrives from the capital announcing Graciliano's return to Rio, he considers this reprieve to be as good as liberty. He wants to regain his personality and again take his place as a member of the human race.

The fourth volume deals with many of the same topics, but a good part of it is devoted to the author's physical and psychological recuperation in a prison hospital. *Angústia* is at last published and, despite Graciliano's misgivings, well received by public and critics alike. Having regained his sexual appetite, and aided by a kindly guard, Graciliano achieves a complete reconciliation with Dona Heloísa. Further, she has obtained a sympathetic lawyer, and successful measures are taken for her husband's release. Graciliano completed all but the final chapter of his memoirs, interrupting his work to attend to other matters and writings. According to his son, Ricardo, he planned a "literary ending," as he had included other necessary observations and conclusions at the beginning and throughout the work. In this ending he would give no more than his first impressions of liberty, not always agreeable ones. Presumably, this would have been the happiest ending possible for the happiest volume by Graciliano.

Chief among Graciliano's preoccupations through the four volumes is the study of the effects of prison life on himself and his fellow prisoners. The problem, whether one considers the larger society that has brought them to prison or conditions in captivity, is that of civilization versus barbarism, one that has concerned many Latin American authors. The problem is found in a variety of forms, and Graciliano examines it from the individual, collective, and universal points of view. The author himself has long struggled to control a violent nature, necessarily repressed as a child subject to harsh parents but inherited from or determined by them. Although he deliberately relaxes restraints on his impatience on occasion, Graciliano is disturbed if he loses his temper.

When a soldier seems first to cheat him of two bananas, then brings him the fruit with a dignified apology, the author is ashamed to have spoken rudely to him. At the same time he doubts that he could behave as admirably as the soldier if their roles were reversed. A similar misunderstanding with his friend Sebastião Hora, a wealthy doctor whose personality has been warped by the drastic change in his style of living, makes Graciliano temporarily feel guilty at having caused Hora annoyance. Reflecting further on the reason for his friend's resentment, a small favor that the author asked hurriedly of him at mess, Graciliano is in turn annoyed. When the vain, excessively formal Hora brings him his food and denies having refused the favor, Graciliano becomes angry. Further complications destroy the friendship between the two overly sensitive, convention-bound men. Although the author realizes that Hora's insistence on certain niceties is out of place, his inability to cope with him and his irritation put him as much at fault. A degree of civility both sincere and appropriate is difficult to maintain under the circumstances. Demoralization of one sort or another is more likely, and consistency in attitudes or behavior becomes increasingly impossible to attain. Graciliano hoards his store of cigarettes, but is highly insulted when he parts with one and the fellow pays him for it. Brute force is sometimes required to perform a kindness, as when Cubano tries to keep the author from starvation. The latter appreciates the intention, but struggles as fiercely as possible against the means. He compares himself with the criminal José, both of them having had a harsh upbringing at the hands of violent parents. But for a measure of education and a natural revulsion to rebelliousness, Graciliano might be like José. Yet the two of them are in prison. Irrational forces seem to triumph. Normally very reserved, the author most incautiously seeks advice of a guard on one occasion, later speaks his mind with a soldier. Concerned about proceeding on instinct, he justifies himself on the basis of many character analyses performed for his novels. Fortunately, his instinct is trustworthy, for reason is not. Perhaps most typical of this confusion that disturbs Graciliano is his apparently successful effort to seem calm and speak rationally with his escorts as they approach the penal colony. His certainty of success under the circumstances strikes him as madness.

The *Memórias* present a gallery of portraits, some sketchy, others well developed, of the many people encountered by Graciliano during his year in prison. Most interesting perhaps are the revolutionaries and their different attitudes. Sérgio is an intellectual Russian with a photographic memory. He amazes Graciliano, not only by reading his novel faster, but retaining the essence of it better than the author himself. He does not bother himself with minutiae, which are what fascinate Graciliano. Nor is he subject to passion, and this troubles the author. Sérgio has suffered terrible torture, yet he does not hate or seek revenge. If he were in power, he would merely favor the most useful and discard the useless, regardless of likes or dislikes. Graciliano is incapable of such stoicism. During a speech before the prison Collective to which he has been elected, the author is faced with the brutal frankness of a stevedore, Desidério. Told that four out of five of his proposals are nonsense, Graciliano must accept defeat. In a rage, he realizes that class distinctions really do not matter; as he himself has shown in *São Bernardo,* it is the position that one attains that makes the difference.

Assessments and comparisons are made of other prisoners. Rodolfo, an Argentinian, has been interrogated at length. His worst torture is the fear that, despite heroic efforts to reveal nothing, the tactics used and fatigue have made him disclose some information. Miranda, it seems, has been tortured also. He likes to show off his bruises, although on closer examination these are slight. The logical assumption to be made, then, is that he is a spy. These two examples lead Graciliano to make one of several close analyses of the fear among prisoners, whether they know any secrets or not, of torture, of interrogation, of possible spies in their midst, and the consequent mutual spying to avoid being spied upon. It is much like a state of war, ironically much like the state of emergency proclaimed and prolonged by the Congress that has put the prisoners where they are.

Studies of collective as well as individual behavior abound in the work. Without leadership the prisoners can do little and are often lacking in cohesion or brutalized. They can only sit and wonder apprehensively what is happening in the next ward, dependent on the rumors and frightening sounds that reach them. In the penal colony they do no more than obey orders brutishly without daring to show any sign of protest or compassion at the horrors about them. On the other hand, when there is organization, the prisoners perform good works for their less fortunate fellows and ultimately for themselves. Able leadership can inspire them to dramatic acts, sometimes worthy, sometimes futile. Effective pressure to bring about action by the authorities to save the life of a prisoner being allowed to bleed to death is useful. Throwing food into the courtyard in order to obtain more eating utensils is of dubious value, except as a show of strength. A hunger strike when the food is adequate seems pointless, especially if it fails. At times the mass is neither inert nor organized, whereupon it may riot. The cause is usually words, their meaning, the need to develop or make them more profound when there is no reason, according to Graciliano's irony. His decision is to remain neutral because, for all their violence, the dissidents soon become friends again and turn against those who interfere.

The author's consideration of civilization and barbarism in prison life involves him in evaluations of many universal problems. As usual, the awareness of a problem comes to him in the form of a specific incident, whereupon he becomes more attentive to similar or related incidents, the persons concerned, his reactions and meditations. One such problem is that of homosexuality, prevalent in any milieu where men have no access to women. One night Graciliano is awakened by desperate cries that turn out to be those of a young boy delivered to the lust of an adult prisoner. He learns that, despite official policy discouraging sexual deviation, homosexuality is very common among the prisoners, and that delinquent boys are often sold to regular inmates. Descrying public ignorance or blindness on this and other vices practiced in prison, and frequently repeating his disgust for sexual perversion, the author continues to make his exposé and analyze his feelings. He describes in detail the behavior of the dominant partner in a homosexual relationship, explaining that his courtship, tenderness, and possessiveness are greater than a man has for a woman. Identifying several "female" members of such partnerships and recognizing in them a number of traits that may make them attractive as human beings, he is nevertheless repulsed by the stereotype that has marked them rather than others. These individuals are fat, soft, given to weeping, and engaged in cooking or laundering. In a discussion of homosexuality, during which he claims as always to try to understand perverts and justify them because of conditions, Graciliano is accused of a lack of objectivity. He cannot excuse and condemn them at the same time, and he admits a bias that may be determined by society in its need for procreation. Yet there is something excessive about his prejudice against physical contact between men, as well as a contradiction in proclaiming his exclusive dedication to women as sex partners. The author cannot bear to embrace a man, or shake hands without washing, even if these are nationally recognized modes of greeting. He declares his entire submission to women, yet states that he has never observed the degree of goodness in any of them that he notes in one of the homosexuals, who nevertheless nauseates him. For all his efforts to dominate them, Graciliano's reactions on this score as on many another are strong, contradictory, and not entirely rational. Witness his extreme apprehension and indignation as the doctor approaches a routine question on army medical reports, and his great relief when, skipping the "infamous question," the doctor shows that he can indeed recognize the difference between normal men and homosexuals.

Before concluding this discussion, I shall refer to an episode of which Graciliano seems justly proud, one where reason does succeed in the end. In the interests of accuracy, however, it must be said that what turns out to be a rational solution starts by instinct. One day in the penal colony Graciliano is approached by Alfeu, one of the most brutal of the guards. He asks the author to prepare a complimentary speech for him to make to the Director of the colony. Extremely fearful, Graciliano reviews a number of points, including situations in the past when he was or might have been truly frightened, concluding that in the present situation he is indeed afraid. He does not see that he can refuse what Alfeu asks, planning only how to do it with the least embarrassment to himself. Yet, despite the probable dreadful consequences, he cannot tell how, the author finds the courage and patience to explain to Alfeu why it would not be suitable for him to compose the speech. Alfeu must do it in his own way for it to mean anything to the Director. Alfeu can understand that Graciliano does not have the same sentiments as he for the Director. The unhappy Alfeu agrees with the author, but is not angry with him. Further, he offers to help him should it ever prove necessary. Graciliano is surprised, relieved, and pleased to have overcome his terrible fear in such a reasonable manner. That he cannot now explain his triumph would indicate a nobler fear at work than that of the pain and humiliation of a beating. If not precisely reason, it was surely a civilizing force and took the form of reason in his persuasion of Alfeu.

CHAPTER 6

Misanthrope or Philanthropist?

I have already discussed in large part Graciliano's fortunes as an intellectual and writer after his release from prison in 1937. Although he produced his most important work after this date, some of his writings give evidence also of a certain negligence or decline in his powers as an artist and thinker. There are a number of short pieces, some of which may be called stories for lack of a better term, and *crônicas*. First written for newspapers or magazines, these were later collected in volumes such as *Insônia*, either in his lifetime or posthumously. Despite their interest for a fuller understanding of Graciliano's evolution, few of these pieces approach the caliber of his major works. Although he seemed concerned and was involved with education, Graciliano's efforts at writing for the young were most unsuccessful. His shortcomings in this field must be partially attributed, at worst to excessive moralizing, of the kind already noted in portions of *Infância*, at best to satirical propaganda, as in some of *Insônia*, in a degree of sophistication beyond the years of his public. The last sizable work of any significance to be discussed here, *Viagem*, embodies some of these characteristics. Shown as failings in this connection, they may be seen also as constants latent in Graciliano's major works, where they are restrained and subject to artistic discipline.

Although he had supposedly been incarcerated for the radical social implications in his writing and his Communist sympathies, Graciliano did not join the Party until 1945. Repeatedly, the author made it clear in his works that he found it almost impossible to admit of generosity or solidarity in real-life society. Only exceptional individuals in extraordinary circumstances could be truly heroic. Fiction might occasionally be stranger than truth, but Graciliano accepted the reverse with extreme difficulty. Still, the ideal existed for him, and he must have entertained some wish to see it materialize. Graciliano had had a glimpse of what groups could accomplish, good, bad, or indifferent, while in prison, but he remained somewhat incredulous when it was good. Given his lack of confidence in any Brazilian social or political system, the humanist could scarcely concede his fellows' rare selflessness as anything but an aberration, whether in art or real life, except in ideological terms.

It must therefore have been with some hope of seeing the particular become universal under ideal conditions that Graciliano, never very eager for glory or adventure, accepted the invitation to visit Czechoslovakia and the Soviet Union in 1952. Without having abandoned his customary skepticism, and often reminding himself and his reader as he writes of his intention to be objective, the author reports that he was shown (or chose to see) chiefly what may be construed as the positive achievements of the Russian system. Here and there the reader finds evidence of Graciliano's crotchetiness, as in the difficulties he first encountered with the President of the Union of Georgian Writers; but cases such as this may be attributed to personalities as much as to genuine objectivity. Although *Viagem* (1954) appears to be little more than a log of notes and sketches, some of them quite unfinished because of Graciliano's untimely death (1953), the form and style are in the main typical of the author. What is new is his general optimism, as though the idealist, despite his reservations, were finally able to express himself because reality warranted it.

Here a brief comparison with Jorge Amado seems to be in order. The latter's early works were rough examples of radical social protest and political propaganda. Having suffered persecution and lived in exile, the mature Amado, a Communist who probably knew whereof he spoke better than Graciliano, preferred to continue to write of Brazil with a new idealism and greater art. Strong indictments of social and political institutions were still to be found. The treatment of the underdog was ever more sentimental. At the same time, Amado's powers as a storyteller grew, as did those of the poet and humorist. Without obviously going abroad for his material, the author tended to create optimistic situations at home in which enlightened Brazilians executed much-needed reforms.

Always quite sober in content and dedicated to art, Graciliano reflected on the other hand a subdued Romanticism sometimes à la Rousseau that seemed to become more pronounced with age. Although civilization as opposed to barbarism was important to him, the author felt also that it corrupted under most sociopolitical conditions. If Fabiano was in some measure Graciliano's "noble savage," his flight from the oppression of the elements and man-made evils of the *sertão* was probably to lead him to the viciousness of a Paulo Honório or a Luís da Silva. Unfortunately, he would not likely find a better fate in a community composed of the Emiles and Sophies that Graciliano seemed to have encountered everywhere in the U.S.S.R.

From time to time Graciliano observes the military in Czechoslovakia and the Soviet Union. Off duty, the soldier in these countries is undistinguished. Like his fellows of the post - World War II generation elsewhere, he hates war. His people suffered terrible losses in the war, and thinking or speaking of them is extremely painful to them. Yet he is fully prepared to fight again, if need be, to defend his homeland and the Revolution. Graciliano witnesses the May Day parade with its well-known show of strength. The speeches delivered on the occasion attest to the Soviet Union's desire to avoid war, however, and popular festivities accompanying the parade underscore the people's love of peace and life.

Like the military, civilians do their part to advance the Revolution, social and cultural as well as economic or political. Everywhere there are school and factory programs, culture palaces, vacation resorts, and the like to improve the lot of the peasant and laborer. Graciliano notes with some astonishment that the elegant Bolshoi theater is maintained for the enjoyment of all. As in everything, the people accept this privilege openly as their right. Professionals, white-collar workers, all those who would be content to be middle class elsewhere, take their turn advancing the cause of Socialism by doing manual labor, while the few who cling to the old bourgeois ways do not prosper. The "individualists" live in slums. The upper middle class waste themselves on high living with prostitutes. Graciliano's first reaction to the former is that their hovels ought to be razed, as should be done in the case of the poor in Brazil; when he learns that they are poor through their own "fault," the notorious nonconformist moralizes on their lack of conformity. These people have the opportunity to improve themselves, after all. As to the degenerate rich, that Graciliano has drawn them according to the stereotype, seen also in other works of his, is obvious.

Especially amazing to Graciliano is the extreme confidence of the majority of Russians in their Revolution and its leaders, for whom they show the greatest and most unabashed veneration. There is no fear on the part of the leaders, and anyone is free to approach them.

Such attitudes are contrary to those of the majority of Latin Americans vis-à-vis their governments and officials, as well as their understanding of the situation in Russia. Graciliano includes moving descriptions of his attendance at the May Day celebration, with Stalin officiating, and a visit with masses of the populace to Lenin's tomb, making constant and invidious comparisons with the circumstances in Brazil.

The small group of Brazilians, Graciliano and his wife among them, are taken on many guided tours in Czechoslovakia and the U.S.S.R., including visits to historical sites that reflect the glory of the Empire. For the Czechs and Russians are proud of their history and preserve its monuments, whatever the period. Graciliano seems to find this pride in a past that the Revolution presumably swept away somewhat curious, and he criticizes the oppressors of the people even if his guides do not. As always, the author is concerned with freedom, personal as well as civil, restrictions thereon, and comparisons between the West as he knows it and the Communist world as he learns of it. He seems pleased, for example, not to be bothered with seat belts and "no smoking" signs on the airplane from Prague to Moscow. Astonished at the magnificence of the subway in the capital, he understands with embarrassment why smoking and littering are strictly forbidden. Personal freedom is permitted if it does not inconvenience others. One must be prepared to be restricted in exchange for favors, as in the case of the old woman whose grandchild is given a seat and fruit to quiet him and who is careful not to let him drop the garbage in the car.

Graciliano is embarrassed equally by the lavish entertainment given the visitors and the constant attendance of guides and interpreters. He is touched but, as always, also a bit uncomfortable at displays of sentiment or affection from individuals and populace, to which he is sometimes exposed. The Russians' generosity and courtesy seem sincere for the most part, but excessive, and Graciliano is assailed by doubts. In order to dispel them, he imagines what people at home will say, that the Communists put up a front for the gullible visitors, et cetera, and he refutes their accusations. As usual, however, Graciliano's temperament does not allow him to be entirely certain of anything, and he conveys the customary ambiguity to his reader. The Russians may be generally attractive and happy with their system; but are they completely honest? Typically, the author deprecates himself, blames misunderstandings on his inability to communicate, especially in foreign languages, and on his suspiciousness. Yet he is constrained to be as good a guest as the Russians are hosts. He tries therefore to obey the laws of hospitality while in the foreign land and also as he writes his log for publication in Brazil. After all, the sentimental journey to the Communist world was almost as perfect in its realization as the ideal of that world had been to the normally sedentary Graciliano.

That he had the opportunity to perfect them doubtless helps to make Graciliano's earlier works very great art in comparison to *Viagem*. Even when one considers the *Memórias do Cárcere,* however, which are incomplete and might have benefited from certain revisions, it is apparent that the breadth and depth of observation, experience, and reflection of Graciliano's memoirs as well as of his fiction give them an authenticity lacking in the travelogue. The greater sincerity of the generally pessimistic works not only renders them more convincing, but may shed further light on the misanthropy that critics have almost universally found in them. It has been made abundantly clear that this misanthropy is rooted in the author's environment, especially in his unhappy childhood, and that Graciliano's art reflects a desire both to conjure and exorcise it.

Incapable of any conventional escape through literature because of his inherent realism, the writer alleviates his suffering and that of others by seeking to understand and give it meaning. Along with his realism in the material sphere, which finds it difficult to deal in abstract time and space, Graciliano practices psychological realism. As a psychologist he must cut across time and space, and thus reaches out to philosophical abstraction. When such abstraction is firmly grounded, however negative its message may seem, it can be helpful to the individual and society. When it is not, and a man of Graciliano's normally pessimistic nature begins to view things in too rosy a light, the lesson can do harm. Fortunately, Graciliano's instincts remain fundamentally unchanged, causing him to hesitate and thereby alert his reader. The misanthropic attitude, like other forms of hatred, may well disguise a disappointed love, a love that hopes to be reborn, and that continues to be philanthropic despite its wounds.

Notes and References

Preface

1. For this chapter I have utilized a number of histories of modern Brazilian literature. I am most indebted to Wilson Martins, *O Modernismo*, in *A Literatura Brasileira*, VI (São Paulo: Cultrix, 1965).

Chapter One

1. "New Perspectives on Graciliano Ramos," *Luso-Brazilian Review*, V:1 (June, 1968), 100.
2. Ibid., p. 93.
3. Ibid., p. 95.
4. *Viagem* (1954), a report of Graciliano's visit to the U.S.S.R. in 1952, seems to be somewhat less impartial, perhaps another case of wishful thinking.

Chapter Two

1. "New Perspectives on Graciliano Ramos," p. 100.

Chapter Three

1. "Philosopher" here is intended to mean a person who has acquired a special wisdom that permits him to deal with life in a more or less consistent, satisfactory way.
2. Although his reasons are different, Adrião would resemble the Prince de Clèves in his death, Luísa might well share some of the Princess' sentiments, and João Valério could be a more honest Nevers.
3. "New Perspectives on Graciliano Ramos," p. 94.
4. *Ibid.*
5. *Ibid.*, pp. 94 - 95.
6. See Graciliano's speech of acknowledgment, *Homenagem a Graciliano Ramos* (Rio de Janeiro, 1943), pp. 19 ff.
7. Osório Borba, "Um banquete absurdo," in *Homenagem a Graciliano Ramos* (Rio de Janeiro, 1943), p. 114.
8. José Lins do Rêgo, "O mestre Graciliano," in *Homenagem a Graciliano Ramos* (Rio de Janeiro, 1943), p. 89.

Chapter Four

1. Morel Pinto's work, to which I have already referred the reader for a more detailed chronology, has proved most provocative in my consideration of Graciliano. I am equally indebted to one of his mentors, Antônio Cândido, *Ficção e Confissão: Ensaio sôbre a Obra de Graciliano Ramos* (Rio de Janeiro, 1956). Many of my remarks on Graciliano's style are derived from Morel Pinto, especially Chapters 1 and 2, pp. 15 - 56.

2. *Caetés* (São Paulo, 1969), p. 160. Further references to *Caetés* (C) will be to this edition. Translations are mine.

3. *São Bernardo* (São Paulo, 1969), p. 218. Further references to *São Bernardo* (SB) will be to this edition. Translations are mine.

4. *Angústia* (Rio de Janeiro, 1953), p. 17. Further references to *Angústia* (A) will be to this edition. Translations are mine.

5. *Vidas Sêcas* (Rio de Janeiro, 1953), p. 109. Further references to *Vidas Sêcas* (VS) will be to this edition. Translations are mine.

Chapter Five

1. Although the term is not to be taken strictly in the Renaissance sense, I should like the reader to recognize that Graciliano's individualism and critical spirit centered on generally human interests and values. At times he even asserted the dignity and worth of man and his capacity for self-realization through reason.

Selected Bibliography

PRIMARY SOURCES

Only *Angústia* (Anguish) and *Vidas Sêcas* (Barren Lives) have been translated. The first is out of print; there have been several editions of Dimmick's translation of the second.

Caetés. 8th ed. São Paulo: Martins, 1969.
São Bernardo. 10th ed. São Paulo: Martins, 1969.
Angústia. 6th ed. Rio de Janeiro: José Olympio, 1953.
Vidas Sêcas. 4th ed. Rio de Janeiro: José Olympio, 1953.
Infância. 3rd ed. Rio de Janeiro: José Olympio, 1953.
Insônia. 3rd ed. Rio de Janeiro: José Olympio, 1953.
Memórias do Cárcere. 4 vols. 3rd ed. Rio de Janeiro: José Olympio, 1954.
Obras Completas. 10 vols. São Paulo: Martins, 1961.

SECONDARY SOURCES

1. In Portuguese

BRASIL, ASSIS. *Graciliano Ramos.* Rio de Janeiro: Simões, 1969. Superficial, but has a good anthology.
CÂNDIDO, ANTÔNIO. *Ficção e Confissão: Ensaio sôbre a Obra de Graciliano Ramos.* Rio de Janeiro: José Olympio, 1956. Short, but profound, study.
CARPEAUX, OTTO MARIA. *Pequena Bibliografia Crítica da Literatura Brasileira.* 3rd ed. Rio de Janeiro: Letras e Artes, 1964. Useful for a relatively complete bibliography of Graciliano's works and secondary sources.
MARTINS, WILSON. *O Modernismo.* In *A Literatura Brasileira,* vol. VI. São Paulo: Cultrix, 1965. This volume has been translated (see below) and is useful for a thorough history of Modernism.
MOREL PINTO, ROLANDO. *Graciliano Ramos, autor e ator.* Assis: Faculdade de Filosofia, Ciências e Letras, 1962. Exploits and enriches Cândido's study.

2. In English

CUNHA, ANTONIO C. R. "Graciliano Ramos: An Annotated Bibliography."

Master's thesis, San Diego State College, 1970. A relatively complete and useful tool.

ELLISON, FRED P. *Brazil's New Novel: Four Northeastern Masters.* Berkeley: University of California Press, 1954. Good, thorough studies of Lins do Rêgo, Amado, Ramos, and Rachel de Queiroz. (Ramos, pp. 111 - 32.)

MARTINS, WILSON. *The Modernist Idea.* Translated by Jack E. Tomlins. New York: New York University Press, 1971.

MAZZARA, RICHARD A. "Gilberto Freyre and José Honório Rodrigues: Old and New Horizons for Brazil." *Hispania,* XLVII:2 (May, 1964), 316 - 25. Discusses some of the tenets of Regionalism; compares and contrasts Freyre's and Rodrigues' views.

————. "New Perspectives on Graciliano Ramos." *Luso-Brazilian Review,* V:1 (June, 1968), 93 - 100. Discusses three of Ramos' novels and contains the germs of my present analyses.

WOODBRIDGE, BENJAMIN M., JR. "Graciliano Ramos." Diss. University of California, 1954. This thesis is listed in the Carpeaux Bibliography, but I have been unable to obtain it.

Index